PANDEMIC PROVERBS
Wisdom for Troubled Times

by
John
Stanko

urbanpress

Pandemic Proverbs
by John Stanko
Copyright ©2021 John Stanko

ISBN 978-1-63360-165-9

For Worldwide Distribution
Printed in the U.S.A.

Urban Press
P.O. Box 8881
Pittsburgh, PA 15221-0881
412.646.2780
www.urbanpress.us

INTRODUCTION

On March 12, 2020, my wife and I returned from a ministry trip to Florida. We picked up our car at the airport, drove straight to a grocery store, did our shopping, and went home to self-isolate or quarantine. The great and terrible worldwide COVID-19 pandemic had just begun. In those early days, we watched television and read online news to learn about this bizarre virus that had brought the world to its knees and, as I write, we are still at home, watching and learning—and still going out once a week to the same grocery store.

I was not content only to watch, however, as this unprecedented event unfolded. I wanted to contribute my insight to the ongoing conversation concerning the implications of the virus and the ensuing lockdown. My emphasis and concern were especially for the Church and its members, and that concern remains today. That is why I began a daily presence online that has not ceased and will not do so any time soon.

About 18 months prior to March 2020, I had experienced what I came to identify as a Facebook revival in December 2018. It was Friday, December 27, to be exact, and I posted a comment on Facebook that got an immediate and enthusiastic response. The feedback was quick and significant enough to capture my attention, so I posted another entry, and then another, and then another. People responded as quickly as I wrote and that went on for three days. When it was all over, I had posted well over 100 entries, and people reported that it gave them the spark they needed to enter 2019. I refer to those three days as a Facebook Revival.

I was careful not to try and do that regularly or to expect that kind of response year-round, for I knew I would wear out my welcome with many of my 'friends' if I did. Yet I found myself conducting another online revival in May of 2019. The response was the same and I filed it away while I continued to advocate for the Church and its members to do more online than we had been doing.

Therefore, when the pandemic hit, I was ready and decided to deploy what I had learned on a daily basis. My presence on social media has been unrelenting and consistent. What you hold in your hand is the result of that decision to have an aggressive presence online, especially on Facebook among my 5,000 friends. This book contains most of my daily posts on Facebook, starting with March 13, 2020—the day after I returned home from Florida.

In addition to social media, I published five books in 2020. I also recorded about 100 Facebook Live sessions, as well as 100 blog talk radio shows (which are podcasts that are part of an online network of shows). My company, Urban Press, published another 12 books for other people, with many more projects slated to be released in 2021. I could list other online programs, classes, and initiatives, but suffice it to say, I was not idle in 2020 while some sat at home and waited.

What You Can Expect

During the pandemic, one of my regular readers wrote to suggest I take my entries and put them in a book format so they would be easier to read. That suggestion intrigued me and the more I thought and prayed about it, the more I agreed with her. I have made no effort to organize my sayings and only edited them for punctuation and clarity. Here are some things you will notice if you choose to read this book straight through (or even if you don't):

1. My objective throughout the pandemic has been to encourage people to take advantage of this time to create and prepare for change. You will see many exhortations for readers to do what is their hearts and do it now.

2. I was clear that God was using the pandemic to get the attention of His people and the Church to make some changes.

3. My call for the Church to reform and change by using

social media not as a last resort or simply to make announcements, but rather as a first means to deliver ministry information and counsel will come through loud and clear. During the pandemic, I released my second edition of *Changing the Way We Do Church: Eight Steps to a Purposeful Reformation*. More strategic, purposeful use of technology is one of the eight steps.

4. In May 2020, the tragic death of George Floyd occurred, which set off a maelstrom of worldwide protests. Since my adult life has been devoted to the ministry of racial reconciliation, you will notice entries that address social justice.

5. You will also notice repeat entries or at least ones with a similar theme. Just as the book of Proverbs has repetitive topics, *Pandemic Proverbs* has the same.

6. You will notice the phrase "Put me in, Coach" sprinkled throughout this compilation. That is a summary of a life philosophy that encourages people to live a bold life and not be afraid of going too far or getting ahead of the Lord. At the beginning of the pandemic, I released my book titled *Put Me in Coach: Living a Bold Life*.

7. There is very little political material, even though it was a presidential election year in the U.S. In fact, if anything,

I emphasized in some of my posts that the Church has become too political and is paying the price for it. Whenever I posted anything remotely political, however, it garnered a quick response, some of it heated. That only served to prove my point and one reason why I stayed and still stay away from politics.

Before I close, let me say a word about the title, *Pandemic Proverbs: Wisdom for Troubled Times*. I chose the word proverb carefully but I need to frame my choice so you understand it. I have had a long-standing love affair with the book of Proverbs. Shortly after my conversion, I was advised to read a chapter from Proverbs every day, reading chapter 10 on the 10th day of the month, chapter 11 on the 11th, and so forth. In that way, I was able to read through the book once a month or twelve times a year.

I loved that practice. I would read, study, categorize the verses into various topical themes, and pray for wisdom as I read. As you are aware, the book of Proverbs contains two-line statements of a truth—not all the truth about a topic of human existence but one that more often than not was and is accurate. Since then, I have written two daily devotional books that focus on Proverbs and have taught on it extensively.

For example, consider Proverbs 14:23: "All hard work brings a profit, but mere talk leads only to poverty." This verse contains a truth but not all the truth about work and wealth. I know some really good talkers and entertainers who are wealthy and then there are some who have worked hard all their lives and don't have a lot of "profit" to show for their effort. This verse contains a kernel or nugget of truth that is often but not always true. The writer was encouraging the reader to work and be diligent and if the reader would do so, in most cases it would be to their benefit and profit. Why do I mention this?

I do so because I found that some people did not consider my short entries proverbs but instead expected or even demanded that they contain all the truth about my chosen subject matter. It fascinated me that I would write two lines of maybe 15 words only to receive back 25 lines with 150 words explaining why my entry was erroneous or incomplete. I knew it was incomplete (I hope it was not erroneous) but was simply hoping to stir up thought and reflection—not produce an essay on the chosen subject. That didn't happen often and I am not complaining. I am only asking that you accept these sayings in this book for what they are—attempts to share some insight or truth on which you can meditate and reflect. I believe what I have included can be of benefit to you in your daily walk with the Lord and relationship with others.

Let me make one last point: Growing in wisdom is work (hey, I think that's a proverb). Obtaining wisdom requires experience, self-awareness, and creativity—and a lot of labor. One must work to extract principles and life lessons from one's successes, failures, and relationships and then reflect on how to connect those principles to other life events. That just doesn't happen, and the wisdom bearer must first *want* the wisdom and then have a desire to share that wisdom with others who could benefit. All that requires effort.

There you have my rationale for the book you are holding in your hand. I am not sure how long the pandemic will last, but I am confident the wisdom in this book will stand the test of time and be relevant long after COVID-19 is history—whenever that may be. Until then, I pray God will use what's contained in these pages to help you gain wisdom which you can then creatively apply to your own life situations.

John W. Stanko
Pittsburgh, PA
May 2021

If I never hear another sermon, I have enough to do and work on until I go home to Him or He returns.

Limit how much TV you watch during this crisis and then use your time effectively; read, study, write, create, live!

Stop acting like the epitome of your spiritual experience is going to church; it's finding and fulfilling your purpose— get busy!

You have claimed you needed more uninterrupted time to create; well . . .

Stop commenting and obsessing on what other people are doing or saying and start commenting on what God is doing in your life!

This crisis is showing us what we need to live but also what we can live without.

"If I write, who will read it?"

If you don't write, no one will.

If slaves could compose songs
under their conditions,
what can you create today with
all that you have?

I am practicing social
distancing but also social
media intimacy!
I want to touch you online as
often as possible.

Your testimony is really not
yours; it belongs to other
people and you have a duty to
share it.

It takes courage to create;
courage is not the absence of
fear, it is learning to function in
the midst of it.

Change your tune from
"Nobody knows the trouble
I've seen" to "Let me tell you
'bout the trouble I've seen—
maybe it will help you."

"By the authority vested in me by the Lord, I hereby pronounce you and your creativity husband and wife. You may kiss your spouse."

A journal of your thoughts/devotions during this time would be a great project to write and publish.

God has hit the pause button and next is the reboot.

We are in the midst of spiritual orthodontics when is God putting things in place to create permanent change in His people.

Stop searching for someone to give you an excuse *not* to create. Look for someone to give you permission. I am such a person.

The way to benefit most from this time is not to deaden your senses through endless entertainment and distractions.

God will extract promises and vows from you in this season that He expects you to follow through on when it's over.

When you change the way you look at things, the things you look at change.

We are holding on until things get back to *normal*, but God wants to establish a *new normal* which represents permanent change.

"When things improve, I will serve Him." No, when you serve Him, things improve.

Be yourself: everyone else is taken.

Then I heard the voice of the Lord saying, "Whom shall I send? And who will go for us?" And I said, "Here am I. Send me!" (Isaiah 6:8.).
"Put me in, Coach."

Paul was in charge of the sinking ship in Acts 27 not because he was a sailor but because he was God's leader. This is the time for leaders who know what to do, not for those who are clinging to what has always been done.

What are you learning to live without in this season that you will *continue* to live without when it's over?

God wants to use your five loaves and two fish to feed others instead of you always looking to eat theirs.

The sailors tried to manage the storm but until they threw Jonah overboard, the storm raged on. And it was in Jonah's best interests to be jettisoned so he could find and fulfill his purpose. This is not the time to give everyone an equal cut to make ends meet; this is a time for change and that requires leadership. It means if you are the one thrown overboard that you accept God has something else for you to do. Holding on to the unessential cargo in a sinking ship was *not* a survival strategy for Jonah or the ship.

God is not asking why you are not some famous ministry star. He is asking why you are not *you*.

Isn't it interesting that God has taken most everything away from us right now *except* social media? That's because He wants us to learn to *use* it.

The new normal is going to be a purpose pandemic when His people all over the world find and fulfill their purpose, instead of watching a few fulfill theirs.

I perform to please an audience of one (God) while I do what I do in front of many.

God has placed the Church on a faith ventilator so we can learn how to breathe in His presence and purpose again.

How do you write your books?" Answer: one page at a time, one day at a time. They do not descend from the heavenly Jerusalem.

Fear is like garlic. We can't smell it on ourselves but others who are free from fear can smell it in an instant.

Very often the testimony you don't want to give is the testimony you *need* to give.

I am using today to get a little better at what I do so tomorrow God can use me.

God wants to deliver you from a place where you are *tolerated* and take you somewhere you are *celebrated*!
Warning: that may *not* be close to your home . . . or it may be across the street.

God does not promote you based on your potential but based on how well you have developed your potential.

GOD: Are numbers and results important in ministry?
YOU: No, obedience not numbers.
GOD: But you tell me you won't create because 'no one' will read, buy, taste, or see it.

Lord, I will do *whatever* you want me to do, as long as it is ...

- in my country
- in my state
- in my county or general vicinity
- in my neighborhood or church
- with people I like, who look and talk like me
- in my church
- on Sunday at 9 and 11 a.m. (unless my kids have soccer, or I just don't feel like getting up or getting dressed)
- inexpensive or requires no out-of-pocket expenses.

YOU: I have labored so hard, and I have no fruit.
GOD: I know, you are in the wrong vineyard. Let me move you.
YOU: But I like this vineyard.
GOD: Come back when you're ready.

GOD: I have called you to ministry.
YOU: I can't preach.
GOD: Who said *anything* about preaching? I have lots of other things for you to do.

YOU: I am not ready. I need more time.
GOD: You are out of time; I am putting you in the game.
YOU: But I may fail!
GOD: There is no failure, only learning.

YOU: I am not ready, God. I need to read and pray more.

GOD: You will never be ready, but I am always ready, so let's be partners.

Old Normal:
I am looking for a job.

New Normal:
I create jobs for others.

YOU: God, I'm afraid. What should I do?
GOD: What you have been doing won't work, so try something new.
YOU: But I'm afraid!
GOD: I know . . . fear not.

Old Reality:
No one will publish my work.

New Reality:
Publish your own.

Old Normal: I consume ministry to feed me.

New Normal: I produce ministry to feed others.

Old Normal:
No ministry will hire me.

New Normal:
I will start my own ministry.

Q: How can I find a job?

A: Start your own company.

You don't *have* to fulfill your purpose; you *get to* do so; but a "have to" mentality will cause you to find all kinds of excuses why you can't.

Fear of COVID-19 is *nothing* compared to the fear of having to rely on God to make a living.

PANDEMIC HEADLINE: God's people are reminded it is better to give than receive and act accordingly.

Don't allow this world at war with a virus to be your excuse *not* to create; use it as your reason *to* create.

PANDEMIC HEADLINE: God's people stop relying on churches to do what they should be doing. They embrace social media as a means to share God's love.

PANDEMIC HEADLINE:
Churches finally enter the 21st century. Use media as a tool to reach people and not just build attendance.

PANDEMIC HEADLINE:
Someone has finally started writing his/her book (take out *someone*, fill in a name—hopefully yours).

PANDEMIC HEADLINE:
God is pruning branches to bear more fruit. Good days of ministry ahead as Church sheds its traditions.

PANDEMIC HEADLINE:
God's people delivered from fear of writing, creating, and serving as God has wanted them to do for years.

PANDEMIC HEADLINE:
God provides for His people in difficult times. He promises to continue doing the same.

PANDEMIC HEADLINE:
Pastors and their people are now preaching every day and not just once a week; also using social media to reach the world.

PANDEMIC HEADLINE: Churches all over the world are flooding the airwaves and social media with good news—*finally*!

PANDEMIC HEADLINE: Prayer has increased during the pandemic. Many more reading and seeking.

PANDEMIC HEADLINE: God is still on the throne, but He is dethroning many things that have stolen His people's strength and focus.

PANDEMIC HEADLINE: God delivers His people from fear. Many stepping out to share their testimonies and encourage others.

PANDEMIC HEADLINE: God has replaced sports/business/glamour/entertainment as the main focus and His people are the better for it.

PANDEMIC HEADLINE: God awakens the Church to the awesome power of technology and social media.

I enjoy when people like my posts, but I am especially pleased when they act on my posts. Faith without action is useless.

It is not important that we hear from the media who have their own agenda. We want to hear from Him and know *His* agenda.

I am not an agent for the media, the antichrist, or politicians. I am His agent and only report on what He is doing.

PANDEMIC LESSON: Social media is an instrument the Lord has given us to fulfill the Great Commission. It is not to be an afterthought, but the main thought.

Don't give the best of your creative and spiritual energy to the media. The news is bad; God is good.

News services change their stories every hour; the Church changes theirs once a week. We need to learn from them and broadcast what God is doing *all* day, *every* day.

What are you counting down toward: the end of your lockdown or the beginning of your new normal?

YOU: You are asking me to give when I have my own needs?

GOD: I will take care of your needs as you learn to take care of others' needs.

Are you thinking new thoughts during the season are you just rearranging the same old furniture in your mind?

YOU: I built this. I love this. And you are asking me to give it up?

GOD: Let's go build something else.

"I have been crucified with Christ and I no longer live, but Christ lives in me. The life I now live in the body, I live by faith in the son of God, who loved me and gave himself for me" (Galatians 2:20)

The cross is more than the declaration you wear around your neck. It is a burden you carry around your heart.

Religion has you carry a cross during Holy Week, Jesus has you carry it *every* week.

YOU: God, I promise I will do 'that' *later*.

GOD: Pick up your cross and follow Me *now*.

Your purpose is the joy that empowers you to endure your cross and despise your shame (see Hebrews 12:1-2).

YOU: But God, this is not what I went to school to do!

JESUS: Pick up your cross and follow Me!

YOU: This cross is heavy.

JESUS: Pick it up and I will help you carry it just like someone helped me.

If your yoke is not easy or your burden is not light, then you have to ask, "Whose yoke am I carrying?" because it's not the one Jesus has for you.

There were times when we thought our flesh was crucified but it had only hibernated to reawaken when someone treated us unfairly.

Your cross is when there is something you want to say along with something He wants you to say and you say what He wants instead of what you want.

You can run from your cross, but it will be waiting for you wherever you go.
Just ask Jonah.

Some of the disciples had to walk away from their family business and what they knew how to do in order to fulfill their purpose; are you ready to do the same?

Your cross is not an inconvenience. It is abandoning your plans to embrace His plans for your life.

Purpose is doing what you love; the cross is doing it where you would prefer not to be, with people you would rather not be with, or for less money than your culture deems you are worth.

The cross is that point in your life where your will opposes His will—and His will prevails.

Don't use the best of your creativity to manufacture excuses about why you cannot fulfill God's will for your life.

When God says fear not, He is actually telling you that you are already afraid.

God is not so much interested in you affirming Jesus' resurrection as He is in you living in the power of Jesus' resurrection. That is the most powerful affirmation of all.

You do good deeds not to earn your salvation, but to prove your salvation. Is there enough evidence to prove you're saved?

After Jesus rose, He had a glorified body and could pass through locked doors, yet He still taught, ate, cooked, and traveled. His resurrection freed Him to fulfill His purpose without restrictions while still being human. His resurrection helps you do the same.

God is love and is motivated by love, so that's why love for your work and love for others is the *only* motivation that will sustain you through dark times and discouragement.

The joy of the Lord is your strength; therefore, if you don't have His joy, you don't have His strength, and your strength is a poor substitute. That's why you *must* be doing what gives you joy, not what gives you money.

Hebrews 12:2 says, "For the joy set before him he endured the cross, scorning its shame, and sat down at the right hand of the throne of God." His joy helped Jesus endure His cross; your joy will do the same.

Today, I don't *have* to be about my purpose, I *get* to be about my purpose; it's a privilege and joy.

We have been taught not to trust our joy because it will mislead us due to the fact that our hearts are wicked. But didn't God promise to give us a new heart? If so, then God will use our joy to guide us to activities that bring us life.

If you believe Christ was raised from the dead, you have what you need to do God's will.

18

YOU: I need a sign, Lord.
GOD: I raised my Son from the dead. If you believe that, you have all the signs you need to receive.

Jesus spent whole nights in prayer. Did He have a prayer list, making endless petitions? He certainly asked but He also spent a lot of time listening. *When you pray, Are you asking God questions? Are you listening for His response? If so, what is He saying? If nothing, then ask different questions.*

Following Jesus cannot be your hobby. It has to be your career.

What could you do today and every day if you were not afraid?

Are you hiding in the bushes of life and busy-ness like Adam and Eve were? If so, it's time to come out and express your purpose and creativity. *No more excuses.*

In Mark 3:21, Jesus' family came to get Him because they thought He had lost His mind. When you follow your purpose, people will sometimes think you are crazy,

When the apostles returned from a ministry tour, Jesus did not send them home to rest; He took them with Him to a secluded place. That's because true rest can only be found in and with Him.

We all need new ways of thinking to help us properly frame our new situations so we can respond properly.

Have you ever wondered what the apostles' families thought about Jesus taking them away to be with Him, especially around the Jewish holy days or for extended periods of time?

Pretending to be small when God has made you big dishonors His will for your life. Release your gift and work to make it all it can be.

God may restore your world to pre-pandemic conditions, but right now, assume you *cannot* go back. What will you do?

You don't need your company's benefits as much as you need the benefits that come from serving and obeying the Lord.

God is not worried or anxious about the future; are you?

We are participating in an event the likes of which the world has never seen. What is your response? Watching TV or preparing yourself for the new normal that is coming our way?

You hated your job, but now that God is trying to reposition you for a new one, you are panicking. Relax, trust Him, and make the most of this time.

What if the devil is opposing you by tempting you to keep everything the same, thus lulling you into a sense of complacency?

Were you *really* that satisfied with your life before the pandemic? Perhaps God is giving you a chance to reflect and change.

Do you *really* think it will be easier for you to do what God wants you to do in five years? *This* is the day the Lord has made, so act now!

God is less interested in you commemorating the resurrection than He is in you living the resurrection.

While "more of you and less of me" sounds spiritual, it's not; what God needs is more of who He intended you to be so you can handle and reflect more of Him.

Telling God you will do whatever He wants sounds good, but if you don't complete the statement by asking "what is it?", you haven't gone far enough.

God can make you a household name and He doesn't need your permission. Don't worship at the altar of privacy; allow God to use you as He wishes.

Your goal should not be to get through this time and be the same person when it's over.

Don't set goals you already know how to accomplish; set audacious goals that will require you to stretch, grow, and learn new things.

God is not impressed by concerts, for He sits in the presence of a good one every day. What draws God's attention is the faith of people who are willing to sing purpose solos for Him and not just watch the performances of others.

In five minutes, Genesis Joseph went from an inmate to the vice president of the most powerful country in the world. God can take you from the bottom to the top in no time once you are ready but only *if you let Him.*

Sunday worship, including travel to and from church, requires two to six hours. The rest of the week is made up of 162-166 hours. Where do you think God wants you to put the emphasis in your life?

Joseph rose to the occasion in Egypt; God is *still* looking for those who will dispense His wisdom in times of trouble. Will you be a Joseph to your generation?

Your world is way too small if you only hang around with folks who look, think, and act like you.

What will you tell Him when He asks, "What did you do during the Great Plague of 2020?"

If you wait until you get paid before you do God's will, then you're a hireling and not a servant.

I write today for an audience of tomorrow.

Of course you don't have any customers; you haven't started your business yet! If you build it, they will come.

Your ideas are like the old negatives that used to come with camera pictures. Those negatives had to be developed—so do your ideas.

The truth will not set you free unless you want it to do so. Until then, a lie will keep you in bondage.

When you denigrate who you are, don't be offended when others do the same.

You are not in a position to negotiate with God; just surrender.

If you are ignorant and God anoints you, all you have is anointed ignorance—even if you are gifted. If you develop your skill and gift and build your mind, then you will have anointed performance. Sorry, there are no shortcuts.

God is calling you; don't let it go to voicemail or put Him on hold.

Go where you're celebrated not tolerated.

Money is not your biggest need before you can do what's in your heart; courage is.

You know what God wants you to do, but you are hoping it will go away. God loves you but He also wants to use you. Give Him your poetry, art, business, or ministry.

God is looking for you, but you may be hiding among the baggage like Saul did in 1 Samuel 10:22-23, even though you know what He wants you to do. What baggage (excuses, past failures, or rejection) are you hiding in?

Stop waiting for God to do what only you can do. That's not spiritual; that's irresponsible. God cannot start your business or write your book. Only *you* can do that or whatever your *that* is.

God has removed the distractions in your life; don't go looking for new ones. Do what He has laid on your heart to do.

Still you do nothing and think, "If I write it, who will read it? If I build it, who will use it? If I paint it, who will buy it?" Stop judging your own creativity before you even produce it. Give God something to use.

Stop excusing your inactivity by saying it's not the right time or season for you to act. Face the fact that you are afraid— pure and simple.

God is not trying to inconvenience His people; He is trying to transform His people.

Jesus was not annoyed by the storm in Luke chapter eight. He was annoyed by the disciples' lack of faith.

Don't try to be any more than God created you to be but, for God's sake, don't be any less. You being any less than God created you to be is unacceptable.

"Truly my soul finds rest in God; my salvation comes from him. Truly he is my rock and my salvation; he is my fortress; I will never be shaken" (Psalm 62:1-2).

Extraordinary times reveal extraordinary people who know an extraordinary God. Consider Joseph, Daniel, Deborah, David, Mary, Paul, and many other heroes of the faith. Why be ordinary when you can be extraordinary?

If you have the ability to impact many, but only touch a few, that is not humility— it is disobedience.

I don't want to be just good; I want to be the *best* and then gather up any accolades and achievements and lay them at His feet where they belong.

The world is running around blaming, fretting, and scheming. God's people are blessing, praying, and sharing.

How can God prove He will deliver you *from* trouble unless He puts you *in* trouble and then keeps His promise?

Your *test* gives you a *test*imony through which you can at*test* to His faithfulness.

Answer Paul's question in Romans 8:35: "Who shall separate us from the love of Christ? Shall trouble or hardship or persecution or famine or nakedness or danger or sword?"

Colossians 3:3: "For you died and your life is now hidden with Christ in God." For something to get *to* you, it has to go *through* Him first.

You are not alone and you are not outnumbered. You and God always constitute a majority.

Your testimony does not belong to you; it belongs to others. That's why you need to share it.

If this pandemic is a conspiracy, I know of only One in the universe who is smart and powerful enough to resist it. That is why I serve His cause and not any other.

God is not punishing you. God is pruning you so you can bear more fruit for Him.

If God is peace and love and He has not given us a spirit of fear, then how can *any* message or insight that foments anger or creates fear be from Him?

"We are going to die!" That has been true since the day you were born.

Our job is not to expose the antichrist. Our job is to glorify the Christ.

I don't care what any antichrist may be doing. I only care about what the Christ is doing. The antichrist has his own prophets. I want to be a prophet of the King.

Jewish zealots were slitting the throats of Roman soldiers while the church was leading those soldiers to Christ. Don't be a throat-slitter; be a Kingdom builder.

"Therefore, since we are receiving a kingdom that cannot be shaken, let us be thankful and so worship God acceptably with reference and awe for our God is a consuming fire" (Hebrews 12:28-29).

The early church thought the end was near, but they did *not* spend time obsessing over what Caesar was doing; they established a rival kingdom called the Kingdom of God and it brought Rome down.

An idol in your life doesn't mean you've turned from God; you just worship the idol along with God.

Procrastination is not the same thing as waiting on the Lord. The first is rooted in fear, the second in faith.

The devil is not your biggest problem right now; *you* are your biggest problem. Get out of your own way and be fruitful.

"I'm not a very good writer, painter, businessperson, speaker." Of course you're not. That's why you need to write, paint, do business, and speak—so you can learn.

Playing small when you are big does not honor God.

While Noah waited on the Lord, he built an ark so he would be ready when God acted. What are you building? If you are only waiting, you won't be ready when the rain comes.

You will make progress only when the pain of staying put exceeds the pain of moving on. Time to choose your pain.

We must be willing to invest in what God has given us to do and not wait for others to do it for us.

I was an associate pastor for 11 years and I preached *two* times. What did I do the other 570 Sundays? I got ready to do what I am doing today. The bigger your purpose, the more preparation time is required.

Waiting on the Lord is good but once you have heard from Him, waiting is not good. It is disobedience. Faith without some kind of action is *dead*.

Waiting on the Lord is not a passive act. It is a time when you aggressively prepare for God to use you while you wait to see how and where that will be.

We tend to repent all day for things we have done, but not so much over things we have not done.

I have a tank full of gas and a closet full of clothes, but nowhere to go. I have embraced my new normal to stay at home and "travel" to other places via social media while I also prepare new material for the future.

In my experience, we are not getting ahead of the Lord; we are lagging pretty far behind. God is able to do abundantly beyond all we can ask or think. Therefore, it's hard to get ahead of the Lord when doing or planning good deeds.

We love to sing *God Will Make A Way* until we have to believe that God will make a way when it doesn't look like He is in any hurry to make a way.

What if God sent you home to teach you how to work in a whole new way? What if you *never* go back to your routine or office? What would that look like for you?

God sent ravens to feed Elijah, manna and quail to feed the Israelites, oil to sustain the widow, and water in the desert for Hagar. You believe those stories, but do you really believe He will do the same for you? It's easy to say yes until you have to trust Him to do so.

When you rearrange furniture in a room, you still have the same old furniture. The same is true for your thinking. You are not doing new things because you are not thinking new thoughts.

What if the income you had before the pandemic never returns? What do you have of value that people will pay you to do? Do you really believe God will provide for you or does the thought of that kind of change or scenario terrify you?

You have as much time every day as the most successful people in the world—24 hours. It's how you use your time that will make you productive and prosperous.

It's true: you are busy. Therefore, it may be necessary for you to *stop* doing some things in order to do new things.

Beware anyone who says, "We will get through this" if they can't describe what the *this* is or what we are getting *through* to. We need wise leaders/not cheerleaders.

Are you busy with the most important things you should be doing, or are you staying busy to avoid doing those important things?

If you are struggling to make sense of this season, here is a word from the Lord: "He who was seated on the throne said, 'I am making everything new!'" (Revelation 21:5). That includes you and His Church.

Joseph told Pharaoh what he should do, not what he had done wrong. God is anointing prophets in this hour, not critics.

Being gracious and merciful does not mean you are ignoring the wrong; it means you understand that mercy triumphs over judgment (see James 2:13).

A rut is a grave with the ends extended. Perhaps you've been in a rut dug by fear; God is here in the season to pull you out and set your feet on a new path.

"Now there were four men with leprosy at the entrance of the city gate. They said to each other, "Why stay here until we die?" (2 Kings 7:3). Those lepers moved out in faith and God provided. He will do the same for you.

Two things immediately attract the Lord's attention: prayer and pride.

Don't expect a parade when you follow your purpose, for others may be threatened by your decision to make progress.

Your job in this season may not be to hear more good teaching, but to find out where bad teaching from your past has factored into your perspective and thinking.

Some are waiting on the Lord like they wait on a bus, so if the bus doesn't come, it's not their fault they aren't going anywhere. If that's you, maybe you are standing at the wrong bus stop?

God gave you your gifts to use; why then would He be offended when you do?

If you think outside the box but stay in the box, then you are still boxed in. Time to burn the box. Just make sure you get out of it first.

If God is raising you up as a leader, don't expect Him to give you a following. You have to go find and create one.

God does not owe you a full explanation before you take your first step; He will reveal Himself *as* you go, not *before* you go.

Purpose is all the endorsement and confirmation you need that God is with you.

You've said, "Someone needs to do something about this or that." Guess what? *You are that someone.*

Why do you keep telling God you're not the one? Isn't that up to Him? If you're the one, don't fight it. Accept it with joy.

A lesson from this season: Don't die with your music still in you. Sing your song! Tomorrow is not guaranteed. Sing it *today*.

Your fear may not be that you will be rejected if you step out; you can handle that. Your fear may be that you'll get a standing ovation. Then what will do you do for an encore?

The less likely of a candidate you are to do what God has put on your heart to do, the more likely you are the perfect candidate to do what's in your heart to do.

Fear, perfectionism, and comparing your work/gift to what others do/have will keep you right where you have always been. It's time to break out and break free.

Zechariah 4:10 (NLT): "Do not despise these small beginnings, for the Lord rejoices to see the work begin . . ." I started a weekly email called the *Monday Memo* in 2001 with eight readers; today I have many more. Don't put off starting what's in your heart any longer.

God's top 10 list of excuses He hears regularly:

1. I'm too old or young,
2. I'm too inexperienced,
3. I'm the wrong gender
4. It's not the right season.
5. I don't have the money,
6. I need someone to support me,
7. My partner doesn't approve of what I do,
8. I'm too busy.
9. My kids are too young,
10. My health's no good.

Which ones are yours?

If God could use Samson, He can use anyone—including you. Your past failures do not determine your future effectiveness unless you allow them to do so.

"Very truly I tell you, whoever believes in me will do the works I have been doing, and they will do even greater things than these, because I am going to the Father. . . You may ask me for anything in my name, and I will do it" (John 14:12, 14).

Our greatest deeds and answers to prayer are often tied to our purpose and creativity, which are God-assigned and directed. He *wants* us to bear fruit!

Prayer is not a one-way ritual. It is a two-way relationship.

Your job is *not* only to pray; your goal is to receive answers to prayer.

"Put me in, Coach!" I will serve on the front lines, the supply lines, or behind the lines.

Paul made tents to earn money, but he never introduced himself as a tentmaker. He introduced himself as an apostle. Don't derive your identity from what you do to make money; identify yourself by what gives you joy and produces fruit for Him and His Kingdom.

Hebrews 1:9 tells us that Jesus was anointed with the oil of gladness or joy. Your joy is the source of your anointing as well. If you have joy with kids, go find some kids. If you have joy with the elderly, go to them. If you have joy giving, then find lots of things to give away. Pretty simple, isn't it?

According to Hebrews 12:2, it was joy that helped Jesus endure His cross and despise its shame. Your joy will serve the same purpose. Therefore, if you have no joy, you have no ability to pick up your cross and follow

The joy of the Lord is your strength, so God wants to connect your work to your joy so you will have His strength to do His will. That's pretty simple, except that we have been taught not to trust our joy because it will lead us to frivolous things.

Your purpose makes you like the burning bush; you will burn brightly but you will never burn out.

You have your work to do and you've probably known for a while what it is. Your job is to do it. God's job is to provide for you while you do it.

Moses went over to the burning bush not because he was called, but because he was curious. When he got to it, God called him. The lesson is to follow your curiosity and what interests you, and you will find your calling.

On a recent morning walk, I saw color, variety, and growth. Those should be the goals in your life right now as well, not to see them in others, but to develop them in yourself.

Your opposition confirms you are moving in the right direction, not the wrong one; consider that Joseph, David, Daniel, Jesus, and Paul had few enemies until they moved in purpose. And often your greatest opposition is from within your own mind and heart—and it's usually fear.

Stop coming off as super-spiritual and in control; you are afraid, so go find and face your fear so you can be free to do and be more.

God is more comfortable with your humanity than you are. Stop trying to change and learn to be yourself.

Your purpose is your mandate for action from heaven. You don't need anyone's permission to fulfill it; *you* are the only one who can stop or limit it.

When you try to be who you are not, you are telling God He made a mistake and should have made you this way or that. Be yourself.

If you are waiting for the perfect song, the perfect poem, the perfect business, the perfect mate, the perfect book, you have set your expectations higher than God's. Perfection is the wrong goal; growth is the right one.

Stop trying to be normal to please others and be yourself to please God.

JOHN W. STANKO

41

Your joy is the guidance system God is using to get you to say yes (free will) to His destiny for your life.

Don't talk yourself out of what you are feeling because it doesn't make clear, logical sense. Listen to your heart.

God is testing you not to show what you don't have but to prove the strength and reality of the work He has done in your life. Stand strong!

Luke 17:5-6: "The apostles said to the Lord, 'Increase our faith!' He replied, 'If you have faith as small as a mustard seed, you can say to this mulberry tree, 'Be uprooted and planted in the sea,' and it will obey you.'" It is not the quantity of your faith that matters; it is the life in the faith you *have* that can do great things.

My job is not to get through this day but to give You, Lord, this day so You can work through me.

I want to be used up when I die and there be nothing left because I wrote it all, read it all, said it all, and traveled it all.

Lord, give me wisdom so You can use me in the days to come. Make me better; make me more like You.

God, the clock is winding down and I don't know how many days I have left; make every one of them count for You and others.

I thank You, Lord, for this season of cleansing and refocus.

Lord, I want to be more God-conscious and less self-conscious. It's about You and Your will, not about me and my needs.

Jesus looked for gratitude when He healed the lepers and was surprised when only one returned to give thanks. Let us be grateful to the Lord today for what we have and what He has done.

Our posts should be filled with gratitudes not platitudes.

This season has come to remind us of our frailty but also to unite the Church, not around politics, but around the King and His Kingdom.

We are all *not* in this together. Yes, the world is united right now by a common experience, but my first allegiance is to the Church and to my fellow believers. My job is to populate the Church and grow God's family, not to recruit people for any other ideology or philosophy.

When is the last time God took your breath away by doing something in response to your faith that surprised you, even though you were looking for it and expecting it to happen?

Ephesians 4:29: "Do not let any unwholesome talk come out of your mouths, but only what is helpful for building others up according to their needs, that it may benefit those who listen." My words and posts are to benefit others and not to vent my anger or share my opinions.

Modern Stanko Translation: Ephesians 4:29 – Do not let any unwholesome talk [Facebook post, comment, or response] come out of your mouths [computer/phone], but only what is helpful for building others up according to their needs [not yours] that it may benefit those who listen [read].

Is your latest testimony fresh, or is it so old that you have to put it under display glass so it doesn't fall apart when you touch it? Time for a new faith journey.

For God to have control in your life, you must surrender. Not talk about it, sing about it, dream about it, schedule it, or read about how others did it. You just need to give up!

YOU: God, if You show me
the new things,
I will let go of the old.

GOD: When you let go
of the old things,
I will show you the new.

If you're stuck, the best way to get unstuck is to ask someone who is unstuck for help so you can be unstuck too.

This is a season to empty your hands so God can fill them with new things.

The post-pandemic world is a new wineskin that requires new wine. You and your purpose and creativity are the new wine.

You are the new thing God is doing.

Today is a good day to start or finish your book, incorporate your business, devise your nonprofit organization, or apply to school!

You may be waiting for God but there's a good chance He's waiting for you, too!

Perhaps more important than knowing what God wants you to do when this is over is knowing what He wants you to *stop* doing.

Money is not your greatest need; courage is!

We cannot return to business as usual when this is over. God sent us home to think about who He is, who we are, and what He wants each of us to do. What does He want you to do *and* do without?

Our goal is not only to have good church, but also to have good deeds done by good people who know their purpose.

I need wisdom to know how I can best finish the work God has given me to do so I can do it boldly and without fear.

Self-pity and serving others are mutually exclusive. If you are engaged in one, you cannot be involved in the other.

Burnout is giving the best of who you are to a situation that gives nothing back. The answer isn't to get healed and then go back into what took your energy. It is to get healed and find purposeful activity that will replenish what it takes, and you will know you have found it when you have *joy*.

Luke 18:40-41: "When he came near, Jesus asked him, 'What do you want me to do for you?' 'Lord, I want to see,' he replied." How would you answer that question if Jesus asked you today? What is your greatest need? And do you believe He can give it to you?

God is using the pandemic to blast you free from the gravitational pull of your past and launch you into the new orbit of your future. It's time to fly higher and go farther.

God anointed King Saul, but they found him hiding in the baggage. What baggage of your past (failure, rejection, fear, relationships) are you hiding in, hoping you won't have to do what you are anointed and appointed to do?

A pre-pandemic activity was watching others fulfill their purpose and express creativity. A post-pandemic activity is *you* fulfilling *your* purpose and expressing *your* creativity.

The birds sing outside my window not because they have an agent, audience, or contract. They sing because they are birds. What should you be doing just because it's who you are, regardless of whether you get paid or have a large audience?

Maturity is knowing and doing what only you can do and trusting God for what only He can do. Immaturity is trying to do what only God can do or trusting God to do what only you can do. I write (what I can do) and trust God for distribution (what He can do). He will not write my books.

My chosen epitaph: "Here lies a courageous man of purpose." For that to be true, it's what I need to be today and every day.

Use these days to establish new habits you will take with you into the new normal: reading, prayer, exercise, creativity, and time to think.

My job right now is *not* to hear from the Lord. My job is to identify my thinking that prevents me from doing what God has already showed me to do. I would suspect you have the same need: not a new word, but a renewed mind.

Perhaps you will not get a *new* word until you obey and take action on your *old* word?

We cannot focus on the new normal—what it will look like and what changes there will be—but we can focus on the God of the new normal who is already there!

Where have you excused yourself from going, giving, speaking, teaching, starting, joining, or leading because *you* determined you weren't ready, were too poor, were too young or old, or had too many family responsibilities?

God is a great communicator. He speaks through circumstances, people who know Him, people who don't know Him, a still small voice, and His Word. If your heart is to hear, His heart is to speak to you. What is He saying?

You have a purpose: something for you to do that only you can do, something for you to be that only you can be. Do you know what it is? Are you fulfilling it?

Like Samuel, our response to these times should be, "Speak, Lord, for your servant is listening" (1 Samuel 3:10).

I want to be like the sons of Issachar: ". . . men who understood the times and knew what Israel should do" (1 Chronicles 12:32).

Advice of St. Augustine: Do what you can and then pray God will give you the power to do what you cannot.

Extraordinary times require extraordinary faith in an extraordinary God from ordinary people.

Prayer of St. Augustine: "Increase my desire for You, God, that I might be able to receive what You are preparing to give me."

The Spirit is in you to give you the mind of Christ. That means you can think the thoughts of God. So, do you have any good ideas?

If God could use Samson, He can use anyone—including you. Your past failures do not determine your future effectiveness *unless* you allow them to do so.

Faith without action is useless. What faith steps can you take today to express your creativity or fulfill your purpose?

Today is the day to set goals you will achieve and plan what role you will play in the post-pandemic world. Don't think small.

You cannot steal second base and hold your foot on first. There is risk involved as you step out, so don't wait for the risk to subside or disappear.

Purpose is the only thing that's too good to be true, but it's true. You get to do what you love as often as possible.

Don't brag that you have had multiple confirmations of a word from the Lord while you still haven't done much with it.

God does not owe you a full explanation before you take your first step; He will reveal Himself *as* you go, not *before* you go.

Jesus called the disciples to stop what they were doing and follow Him. He gave them no indication of what was ahead because He called them to a relationship, not an occupation. The same may be true for you.

YOU: I need a job.
GOD: Start a business.
YOU: That's too big for me.
GOD: Don't shrink your world to fit your current size. Get bigger so you can handle more!

Mary asked *how* she could be pregnant. Gabriel told her through the Holy Spirit. You ask *how* you will do what is in your heart. You get the same answer.

God wants to lead you to a land flowing with milk and honey instead of the desert where you get bread and water. Your choice.

Your objective is the new Promised Land, not the old Egypt. If you choose Egypt, you will instead wander in the Wilderness.

Open my eyes today, Lord, to see the opportunities around me and my role in seizing them for Your purpose and glory.

Most don't know their purpose because they have never asked; some never ask because they are afraid—afraid they may discover it and then be responsible to *do* it.

Proverbs 14:28: "A large population is a king's glory, but without subjects a prince is ruined." You are comfortable with being small, but can you grow to be just as comfortable with being big?

God invests in us and wants to see a return on His investment.

God, make me a good and faithful steward of the message You have given me. Help me focus on who I am and what I do to proclaim Your truth in the power of Your Spirit through the gifts You have bestowed.

Lord, I want to be Your purpose ambassador to as many nations as possible. Expand my borders and increase my capacity to love and learn.

GOD: "Who will go for us?"

ISAIAH: "Here I am, send me!"

Mark 12:37: "The large crowd listened to him with delight." *Lord, give me something to say and help me say or write it in such a way that it holds people's attention, imparts important truth, and gives them delight.*

May the Spirit of Isaiah come upon you today. "Put me in, Coach!"

John 15:16 — "You did not choose me, but I chose you and appointed you so that you might go and bear fruit—fruit that will last—and so that whatever you ask in my name the Father will give you." Where's your fruit?

So you really think more time is what you need before you start your business, publish your book, go on a missions trip, or launch your ministry? You don't need another sermon, you need to overcome your fear and say, "Put me in, Coach!"

When Nehemiah heard the report of Jerusalem's plight, he fasted and prayed, but when the king asked him what was wrong, he said, "I'm ready. Put me in, Coach!"

God, I don't want to have an ordinary week, but rather an extraordinary one in You and Your service.

When David saw Goliath, he did not wait for an invitation or confirmation. He said, "I'll fight. Put me in, Coach!"

Lord, I need Your help this week. There are so many opportunities to serve You and others. Give me strength, wisdom, and alertness.

God, if You are looking for someone to use this week, my prayer is, "Put me in, Coach!"

I am reading the apocryphal book named Ecclesiasticus. It says in 4:31, "Do not keep your hand open to receive and close it when it is your turn to give."

God is love so any work you do not motivated by love cannot be from God, Think about that.

If you do what you do only for the money, no matter how noble the task, the Bible calls you a hireling. Do what you do for love and don't hire yourself out to the highest bidder.

Fruit is always measurable— pound, bushel, cluster, peck, and orchard. So . . . what and where is your measurable fruit?

God has provided for His people through a raven, a ram, a fish, manna, and quail; there is no limit to how God can provide for you. Do God's will (your job) and let Him provide as He chooses (His job).

Ask yourself, "What would I do if I had all the money I needed to live?" If the answer is *not* what you are doing now, then you may be in the wrong place.

If you continue to belittle your purpose or gifts, don't be surprised or offended when others do the same.

I wonder, if when we are bored in church, prayer, or some other activity where there is no life, is God bored too?

Persecution hit the Church in Judea, so they went out to Samaria and found out God was with them. Fast forward 2,000 years. A pandemic hit the Church worldwide, so it went out on social media and found out God was with them.

Church should not be a ritual, but a place where you go to celebrate your victories with Him and others and get your tanks filled and your engine tuned for new adventures.

God, I need to stop doing some things, even though I enjoy them, to do other newer things. Time to release and move on.

"Good church" is like a sugar high; it feels good but doesn't last long before you find yourself in need of another fix. God wants good church but also good people who go forth to serve others.

When we consume the Word without an outlet to apply what we've learned, we become overweight believers, addicted to receiving but anemic toward giving.

It is remarkable that God has sent the worldwide Church home to ponder what it means to be the Church.

Denying you can do something and do it well, when in actuality you can, isn't spiritual or humility; it's a lie.

If you've known the Lord for 20 years, you've heard at least 800 sermons, not including conferences, special events, books, recordings, radio/tv/internet. You don't need another sermon; you need the courage to apply what you know.

Playing small when God made you big isn't spiritual; it's foolish.

I am a good writer and a not-so-good pastor. Therefore, where should I spend my time? Trying to be who I'm not or being the best *me* I can be?

Time to take the burqa off your spiritual self and show forth the beauty and magnificence of who God made you to be. No more false humility.

You cannot sing your song if you are sitting in the audience. Time to take your place on the stage and show what God has done is your life and allow Him to work through you to bless others.

You assume everyone sees what you see: the need, the opportunity, the problem—but they don't. You see it because it's part of your purpose and because God wants you to act on what you see. Don't wait for others to lead. Step up and out to do it yourself.

If you asked others to invest in your company but refused to do so yourself, the investor would decline. Yet you want others to invest in your development when you don't invest in yourself. Spend some money and time to make yourself better at who you are and what you do.

The only power Daniel had in Babylon was the power of his purpose, but that made him the most significant man in the kingdom. Your purpose will make you a leader wherever God assigns you. That's why you *must* study leadership.

If you continue to belittle your purpose or gifts, don't be surprised or offended when others do as well.

You should use social media not to share trivial things but to broadcast your testimonies and insights that can impact, inspire, or encourage others. You should also consider having other outlets, like books, blogs, and videos to which you can direct people.

I don't care what you are going to do this year, I want to know what you are going to do today that contributes in regard to what you are going to do this year.

●●●●●●●●●●●●●

Get a job that does not require all your life energy so you can pursue your business or ministry dream. Think of it as your tent-making activity like Paul had.

A key to being in business for yourself is having multiple streams of income so if one stream fails, you have another. My streams are publishing, fundraising, teaching, consulting, and speaking. Think bigger than you are thinking now and pray, "Put me in, Coach."

If your creativity is a gift, then it cannot be a hobby; it must take center stage in your life's performance.

Faith is like a muscle; the more you use it, the stronger it gets. You need some faith exercise!

You don't need more people in your life who will commiserate with your small thinking. You need some people who will punch you in your spiritual gut and take your breath away.

Being gracious and merciful does not mean you are ignoring the wrong; it means you understand that mercy triumphs over judgment (see James 2:13). God has extended mercy to you and expects you to do the same to others.

What did you do as a child that you no longer do but could hold a clue to your purpose?

Growing older should increase your capacity to bear both truth and the pain of others.

Deciding things are going to be different in your life is good but not enough; you must set some stretch goals and have someone hold you accountable or else you will revert to your old habits, which will produce the same old things in your life.

No race, gender, culture, nation, person, political party, generation, or occupation has cornered the market on sin; all are guilty before God until they put their faith in Christ.

I don't want to be a talking head pointing out problems. I want to be a walking witness of the only solution there is for every problem known to man: faith in Christ.

I avoid most of culture's labels for our current problems. The root cause of killings, thefts, abortion, racism, sexism, and any other -ism you can think of is sin. Therefore, unless we deal with the root, the plant will continue to thrive. The Church is the only one with the solution to sin: the Cross.

My life has been devoted to reconciliation, first reconciling people to God and then to one another. I use words when needed, but I model a life yielded to serve those who do not look or think like me as the essence of my gospel.

God may have you be a part of a solution to a problem you did not cause. If you refuse, you will become part of the problem.

Racism manifests as a cultural problem but it is a sin problem. Its roots are in the Garden when Adam and Eve fell. We must address it from the perspective that all have sinned and fallen short of the glory of God.

David served the people while Saul was running around acting crazy. Yet David never criticized Saul and even did Saul's job while Saul used God's army to pursue David. *God, don't let me give less to my leaders, church or civic, than David gave to his.*

62

Joseph was the leader in Egypt not because he pointed out what was wrong but explained what needed to be done today to get ready for tomorrow. Right now, there are a lot of critics but not enough leaders. God, make me a leader!

There is more joy in giving and more comfort in trusting the Lord than an increase in our bank accounts, wealth, or retirement funds.

In Exodus 31, those who did creative work with their hands did not do so as a hobby or side interest; they did it as a calling from God. Treat your creativity the same way.

The Spirit of God is in you to give you the mind of Christ. Why are you so surprised that you have it? That means you may be thinking the very thoughts of God for your life.

One person operating in purpose is more powerful than 20 people who are hired but not called.

We do not serve a human economy; we are in God's transcendent economy. Stop playing by the world's rules and play by God's.

"What if what I am thinking is not of the Lord?"

A better question: "What if it is?"

If you are walking a new road, don't listen to a guide who has not traveled that road.

If you've had something in your heart to do or be for many years, I can say with confidence that it is not you or the devil. Overcome fear and stop doubting.

Your heart is private property. No one can trespass there and tell you what should or should not be in it. That role is reserved for God.

Do not surrender your purpose dream to someone who has a smaller dream than yours. They may try to shrink yours down to match the size of theirs.

The thing about your potential is that you don't know its size until you start to pursue it. Don't limit yourself by fear of going too far.

The Dead Sea is dead because it has no outlets. It always taking in, never giving out. There's a lesson there for you and me.

We love each other not because we are worthy or have a choice; we love because the King commanded us to do so.

Your purpose is your joy; your cross is your humility.

Study the church and you get rules; study the Kingdom and you get life.

I owe allegiance to the Kingdom above country, race, denomination, culture, tradition, or family.

The Kingdom is not a democracy; we don't get a vote, only a voice.

Isaiah 6:9 — Then I heard the voice of the Lord saying, "Whom shall I send? And who will go for us?" My response is "Put me in, Coach! I'll go." How about you?

Church is with you a few hours a week; the Kingdom is with you everywhere you go and regulates all your life and behavior.

Your purpose is a Kingdom matter, not a church matter; therefore, you have an obligation to find your purpose expression whether your church can provide you an outlet or not.

It is not about what church you are in, it's all about what kingdom you are in.

Anyone can learn how to behave a few hours a week for church; it's more important to learn how to live 24/7 in the Kingdom.

Since I am a citizen of the Kingdom, the King rules my mouth, social media presence, behavior, attitude, and life's work.

The kingdom of God was Jesus's singular focus; it should be ours as well.

You have "crazy makers" in your life who want you to play a supporting role in their drama. You must resist their efforts.

"I think I'll go back to what I was doing."

The key words are: *go back*.

Time to move forward, not go back!

I dare you to get 'ahead of the Lord' by expressing your purpose, doing good deeds, and being creative.

If you are ignorant and God anoints you, don't think the anointing will overcome your ignorance.
Do the work.

God is not offended when you step out and act on what you see, hear, and think.

Time to trade in your spectator tickets for a uniform and get in the game. "Put me in, Coach!"

God is releasing the 2.0 version of you after this crisis; He is upgrading all your systems, too.

Shakespeare said the world's a stage, but it's where you should be authentic and not act like someone you're not.

When you change the way you look at things, the things you look at change.

Your purpose is your spiritual set of fingerprints; you should leave a distinct mark on whatever you touch.

A new you among old friends is not always recognized or appreciated. Is it time for some new friends?

When friends and family are not supportive of what God wants you to do, then you often need to invest less time and energy with them, while still loving them. It's called setting boundaries.

Beware of anyone who counsels that we just need to "get back" to anything; God isn't a "get back" God; He is a "move on" God.

You will make progress only when the pain of staying put exceeds the pain of moving on. Is it time to move on yet?

Some think spirituality dictates that if God is in it, it will all go smoothly from the start. That's not accurate. You must be willing to learn from your mistakes, even when God leads you to do something.

"I am posting, creating, and/or broadcasting but no one seems to be paying attention." First, you don't know that for sure and second, you have to earn your audience through helpful, consistent material. Stay the course and keep getting better at what you do.

This time is a defining moment when you get to rewrite your life script; don't play a bit part—choose a lead role!

Your comfort zone can also be your danger zone.

In two months, the world has become a different place, so the new future will require you to be a different person.

The Dead Sea is 'dead' because it has so many minerals but no outlet. You will be the same if you only take in God's blessings and don't find a way to share them with others.

James 1:19 — "Everyone should be quick to listen, slow to speak [or write] and slow to become angry." I looked up the Greek word for *everyone* and it includes you (and me).

My books are not part of the heavenly Jerusalem; they do not descend from on high. I write them one page at a time, one day at a time. Stop over-spiritualizing what God has given you to do. Face your fear and get going.

Hurt people hurt people. If you want to be a healer, then you must allow God to heal your own pain.

The world does not need another sermon right now; it needs you in the fullness of your purpose and creativity; stop listening and start producing.

There is an increase in which God is interested but it isn't the abundance of possessions. It is an increase of love practically expressed first to the household of God and then to the world.

Procrastination is not the same thing as waiting on the Lord. The first is rooted in fear, the second in faith.

You don't want *more*? Sorry, it's not your choice. Jesus said to those who have, more will be given, so to resist the more in your life is to resist God.

Rebekah went to the Lord in Genesis 25:22 to ask, 'Why is this happening to me?' and God answered her. That's a good prayer for you in this season; you should expect an answer too.

It is possible to be sincere but sincerely wrong. Sincerity does not sanctify ignorance or opinions.

Somehow we got the mindset that we were to evaluate and consume ministry rather than produce ministry.

Criticism and nitpicking are not gifts of the Holy Spirit. Your job is not to find fault but to encourage, not to judge the work of others but to produce your own. Where's your fruit?

Who made you judge and jury of your own creativity? If it blesses others, then what right do you have to shut it down or refuse to produce it? The proof of the pudding is not in the making, but in the eating.

God does not want you to maintain your world, He wants you to expand your world. Do you have a maintenance or expansion mindset?

I can use a computer to edit, but I cannot hire one to produce the kind of creativity that's in you. Time to move out of edit mode and move into create mode.

It is ironic that some people work to obtain health benefits, then jeopardize their health by doing work they loathe.

God cannot change you into the person you are pretending to be. The goal is not adaptation; it is transformation.

"I am a creative person." That declaration and realization changed my life 15 years ago. "God has not given us a spirit of fear" set me free to express my creativity. "Emmanuel, God with us!" empowered me through a creative partnership with God.

Give yourself permission to be who God made you to be. No need to apologize to anyone.

The Bible paints a picture of the Spirit clothing Himself in you. He puts you on as a garment and moves about, so when people encounter Him, it is through you. That means He is comfortable with your humanity as you are, not as you think you should be. Be yourself.

It is not God's will that you are bored with your work life, dreading to start and anxious to stop. God is using your boredom to tell you something.

Your creativity is expressed in how you dress, encourage others, arrange your work area, address a difficult or angry person, or counsel others. You are a creative machine. Don't fight or judge it; just release it and be you.

Creativity goes beyond writing, painting, or music. It is evident in solving problems, raising children, shaping business, expressing ministry, managing time. You are creative and the best of your creativity is yet to come!

The same Spirit that raised a dead man back to life dwells in you. You have divine power working in and through you.

The Creator has made you creative in His image. Your creativity is not to be a sideline or hobby; it is to have a lead role in your earthly performance.

Jesus calls you to repent, which means to change your mind, for the Kingdom is at hand. Repentance is not an event but a lifestyle in which you confront your thoughts that cause you to be out of alignment with the King and His Kingdom.

When people touch you in your purpose, they are touching an aspect of God He has entrusted to your care and expression.

Repent or change your mind that all you need is another word from the Lord. You need to fulfill the words you have but have chosen to ignore due to fear.

Repent or change your mind that all you need to do is go to church, give some money, and stay out of trouble. You have a purpose to fulfill and creativity to express.

Repent or change your mind concerning your fear that you can go too far or do too much for God.

Repent or change your mind that all you need is a Holy Spirit breakthrough. You need to prepare for a breakthrough or you will mess it up or miss it when it comes.

I am a writer, so I write. Who are you and what do you do? How can you do more of it?

Repent or change your mind that God needs an organization to provide for you. He can use one, but He doesn't need one.

We are so concerned about going too far that we often don't go far enough, thus never exploring the furthest boundaries of our purpose and creativity.

If I never hear another sermon, I have enough to do and work on until I go home to Him or He returns.

Limit how much TV you watch during this crisis and then use your time effectively; read, study, write, create, live!

Stop acting like the epitome of your spiritual experience is going to church; it's finding and fulfilling your purpose—get busy!

Study the entire Word but choose one book you will read and study again and again. Become an expert in that book. For me, it was and is Proverbs.

Stop commenting and obsessing on what other people are doing or saying and start commenting on what God is doing in your life!

The Word without your gift is academic; your gift without the Word is dangerous. The bigger your gift, the greater your need to be grounded in the Word.

The best indicator of purpose is joy. What do you do that gives you joy you cannot explain or ignore? That is not a trick to mislead you but rather a road sign to direct you.

Purpose is what you gravitate toward doing and being even though there may be no money in it for you. What would you do if you had all the money you needed to live on? The answer is an indication of your purpose.

You never have to go looking for purpose. It always comes looking for you. What situation or group of people always seems to find you and you have the answer to their problems?

Jesus had a clear purpose statement: "to seek and save the lost" (Luke 19:10). Paul's was to take the gospel to the Gentiles. My purpose is to create order out of chaos. Do you know what yours is?

Israel wanted a king to "fight their battles." It is still a temptation to want someone we can watch fulfill his (or her) purpose so we don't have to fulfill ours.

David had an encounter with God and, when Israel needed him, he then volunteered to fight the giant. The difference between David and Saul was one dealt with his fear, the other succumbed to his. Time to choose who you want to emulate: Saul the coward or David the

King Saul had all kinds of supernatural encounters with the Lord, yet when they needed him, he was hiding amongst the baggage. It doesn't matter how many touches from God you've had. If you don't deal with fear, you will hide from your purpose and creativity just like Saul did.

The scoreboard clock for my life is ticking down. I cannot see the time left, but I know I am in the fourth quarter. That is why I seek to make every day count. Stop assuming you have all the time in the world. You only have today.

I write, God provides the readers. You do your part and I promise you God will do His. You don't, He won't

If God is the light in your life, it's time for you to take the bushel off and let Him shine through you.

I don't pre-judge my creative ideas. I act on them and allow God to sort out which ones He chooses to use.

You should fear the Lord if you are considering robbing a bank, not if you are doing good deeds or structuring your life to do more.

God stopped the sun for Joshua to finish his work. You trust the Lord for money and ministry. Learn to trust Him for time— not more, but to effectively use what you have.

Lord, I freely offer my gifts and experience today to serve others. Open my eyes to the opportunities around me.

"I'm too busy" is a convenient excuse to cover fear; the simple solution is to get un-busy.

If there is no joy, even when you do something well or important, then have the courage to stop.

If you write two pages per day, for example, you will have 60 pages in a month. Don't wait for large chunks of time that will never come. Learn to create bit by bit.

Jesus used parables, which were creative ways to present God's truths. *Lord, give me similar creativity that will convey Your love and gospel to this generation.*

A hard heart stops feeling, a stiff neck loses flexibility, and a closed mind ceases to entertain new thoughts. Any one of those is critical, all three are fatal.

* * * * * * * * * * * * *

Lord, I have prepared and trained but I put all that in Your hands. You know I still have much to learn, but this is where I am right now so use me, Lord. If You keep me on the bench today, then let me cheer on those who play until my prayer of "Put me In, Coach" is answered.

Lord, give me more insight, better ways to say what You want me to say, and a bigger audience. "Put me In, Coach" and let me show off what You have done in my life to a large crowd.

Lord, I ask for more insight, more wisdom, more creativity, more power, more influence, more opportunities, more ways to touch more people. God, I guess you get the idea that I want more because I believe more is Your will. I leave all that in Your hands now as I go about my work.

God, You have put me in the game to write. I trust You to guide my thoughts and give me insight and the ability to communicate it to Your people. No fear, Lord, no fear.

Lord, I trust You for time. I have many things to do, but I ask that You guide my steps, give me wisdom, and help me do more than I thought possible through Your power that works in and through me.

Social media is my pulpit and my friends/followers are my flock. I have no authority in their lives apart from influence via regular posts with content. I preach all day every day. "Put me in, Coach."

Lord, take what I write and say every day, and use it to stir, encourage, challenge, direct, inspire, correct, and/or bless Your people all over the world.

Ecclesiasticus 11:25: "Hardship is forgotten in time of success and success in time of hardship."

I want to be creative in what I say on social media but also innovative in how I use it. Give me wisdom, Lord.

Success is doing what you love as often as possible; money is a byproduct not a destination.

I am not only creative in how I express my work, I am also creative in how I organize my work. Chaos will drown your creativity if you are not careful.

The pandemic has reminded us that the end is always near for every one of us.

The disciples were more fearful of the calm after the storm than the storm itself and the same may be true for you. The storm gives you an excuse not to create; when it ceases, then you have to be who God made you to be.

I am positioning myself to have a significant role in the post-pandemic world as God allows. "Put me in, Coach."

I would rather fail three times than wait to get something perfect, for my three failures will contribute more to its ultimate perfection than my waiting.

The pandemic has taught us that technology can enhance and even initiate relationships, but we still need the touch of those we love every now and then.

We have tanks full of gas and closets full of clothes and nowhere to go. The pandemic has taught us that life is not found in an abundance of possessions or activities.

The pandemic has shown us how fragile we are and how powerful God is.

The higher your calling, the deeper your preparation.

You have prayed for money, but God gave you an idea instead. When you cash in the idea, you will have the money you need.

The pandemic has taught us that tomorrow is not guaranteed; do it today.

God made you a creator, not a critic; an encourager, not a judge; a river, not a dam.

Perhaps you are disturbed because you are 'disturb-able.' Don't give causes and people access to your heart. You are to guard your heart, not make it a thoroughfare.

The world has never seen the likes of you, so stop trying to be like someone else. Be true to who you are.

The world is listening for your music; don't deprive it by holding back who God made you to be. Sing your song.

Joy is the best indicator of purpose; love is the best motivator to express it.

Bezalel in Exodus 31 designed art for the tabernacle that was only seen by the High Priest and God; are you also willing to create for an audience of a few?

You cannot be what you do not see. Ask God for a vision for your life and then work to fulfill what you see.

Sometimes you have to get rid of old things before God will give you new ones. Time to clean house.

If you rearrange the furniture, you still have the same old furniture. The same is true for your old way of thinking. Time for some new furniture in your heart and mind.

John 7:17: "Anyone who chooses to do the will of God will find out whether my teaching comes from God or whether I speak on my own." Commit to do the will of God *before* you know what it is and He will show you what it is.

Jesus said, "You shall hear of wars and rumors of wars" (see Matthew 24:6). A rumor is nothing more than fake news. Don't fall for fake news; put your hope in the good news.

Purpose work makes you like the burning bush. You burn brightly but are never consumed. Non-purpose work burns you up and out.

I wish someone could pray for you, you fall down, and get back up with a PhD. Unfortunately, that's not how it works. God will help you, but He won't do the work for you.

Lord, Your people groan and need Your help.

Maturity is unlearning what you previously learned that is now hindering you from maturing.

Paul's admonition is important to remember as we face these times: "Do not be overcome by evil but overcome evil with good" (Romans 12:21).

I am not into talking anyone out of what they are feeling right now. I am happy to hold their hand and empathize as best I can.

We must address the ills of society without being consumed by those ills—or our anger

To succeed in your purpose, you have to read and study the Word while others watch the news.

They accused Jesus, the sinless Son of God, of being in cahoots with the devil but He turned it into a teaching opportunity. No need to take so many things personally.

Some people have so many 'pet' peeves they could open a zoo. Time to chill out and lighten up.

Philippians 3:14 – 'I press on toward the goal to win the prize for which God has called me heavenward in Christ Jesus.' Press on = something is opposing you; goal/prize = be specific; called = what has God put in your heart to do?

"But by the grace of God I am what I am, and his grace to me was not without effect. No, I worked harder than all of them—yet not I, but the grace of God that was with me" - 1 Corinthians 15:10.

God never apologizes for what you go through but promises to always go through it with you.

Go where you're celebrated not tolerated. It's God's way of showing you where He wants you to be.

Until we are committed to broadcast instances where racial reconciliation is taking place, we cannot combat the images of hatred that dominate. We must use the power of our media to show that in Christ there is at least the potential for harmony and peace.

The mob chose Barabbas, an insurrectionist, over the Prince of Peace. The mob still tends to make the same choice.

Racism is a stronghold with a strong hold on people's minds and hearts. There is only one way to deal with a strong hold; pull it down through spiritual means. Second Corinthians 10:4 says, "The weapons we fight with are not the weapons of the world. On the contrary, they have divine power to demolish strongholds."

Your creativity is not a hobby; it's to be expressed as often as possible. When you do that, you honor the One who gave it to you.

In the midst of a pandemic, with brutality and racism rearing their ugly heads and corruption all around, the message of Jesus still rings forth: "Repent, for the kingdom of heaven is at hand" (Matthew 3:2).

My publishing company has 50 authors: 26 people of color, 24 white. I have offered my services to all, some who could pay, others who could not. I know that seems insignificant in light of current events, but I have offered my life and gifts as a means to reconciliation and will continue to do so

I have given my adult life to do what I could on an individual basis to combat racism; I have aligned myself with churches that have stood for that value. I will continue to do all I can to stand with people of color everywhere and devote my gifts and presence to their healing as my equals.

The message of the Kingdom cannot be mixed with the message of our culture. We must address racism at a cultural level, but only God can change hearts. For that, the church needs to model and preach reconciliation, being an ambassador of Christ, not independent agents.

"All this is from God, who reconciled us to himself through Christ and gave us the ministry of reconciliation: that God was reconciling the world to himself in Christ, not counting people's sins against them. And he has committed to us the message of reconciliation" (2 Corinthians 5:18-19).

"Put me in, Coach" where I am needed the most. I don't just want to play the game. I want to win the game wherever You choose to deploy me. I am not content to sit on the bench but know I must bring my 'A' game every day to get better at what You created me to do.

Lord, I present my gifts to be used as You see fit. I lay them at Your feet—my writing, humor, teaching, wisdom—and pray that together we can utilize them all to be a blessing in the lives of my friends and family today.

Lord, open my eyes to the opportunities to make a difference, and grant me empathy to feel what others feel without having to be told. Let me be proactive in doing good and not reactive to the evil prevalent in the world.

Jesus had not much to say to Pilate (Rome), nothing to say to Herod (the local politician), but He had a whole lot to say to the religious leaders.

Lord, use me today to bring healing to the broken, direction to the wayward, peace to the confused, wisdom to the seeker, joy to the downtrodden, and relief to the oppressed.

I have received so much grace from the Lord and that is why I have to season what I do and say with the same grace.

I've seen and heard some church folk who have a lot of mess in their past talk and act in a way that tells me they have forgotten their past.

I am not only wearing a face mask but also sackcloth and ashes. This is a time to humble myself before the Lord and wait on Him.

Why don't governments change that much when new people come to power? It's because the new people overestimated their goodness and their immunity to the abuse of power.

We have a leadership crisis in government's house, but also in God's house, and the latter is where God's judgment begins (see 1 Peter 4:17).

Leadership is not learning how to wield power; it is learning how to give it away to empower others.

"If I was in charge I would do better" sounds good, but unless you prepare yourself now to be the kind of leader you want to be, you will be just like the leader you opposed and replaced.

I've seen people repent of sexual sin and financial improprieties, but I've never seen any leader repent of abusing power. Power is the most intoxicating force in the universe. Unless you determine what you will do with power before you get it, I can assure you that you will abuse it once you have it.

Every act of racism is an abuse of power: the desire to dominate, to suppress, to feel superior by making someone else inferior. The point I have been making for years is that no one is exempt from this tendency and we must all take measures to guard against its reality.

We assumed that once people became leaders, God would give them the wisdom to lead. That is not the case any more than making someone a doctor would automatically give them the ability to perform surgery. We need to get better at leadership and that is not a quick fix.

I've seen people oppose tyrants and get power, only to become worse than the tyrants they opposed. The only antidote for power is servant leadership. Without service, leaders, even in the church, believe they deserve their role and the honor that can come with it. When that happens, everyone is in trouble.

There is no braver thing to do than to be yourself when everyone around you wants you to be someone else.

Lord, I owe You. You have been good to me and mine, so I am reporting for duty, to serve or not, to speak or not, to write or not. "Put me in, Coach."

What you need is not more insight, but more courage to carry out the insight you have.

In times when you have little control over external things, you still have a say over your own personal development and growth.

Don't ever worry about being outnumbered or outvoted. You and God constitute a majority wherever you go.

You have a purpose: something for you to do that only you can do, something for you to be that only you can be.

Isaiah 59:19b: "When the enemy shall come in like a flood, the Spirit of the Lord shall lift up a standard against him." I would say the waters are pretty high right now all over the world.

"Freedom is never voluntarily given by the oppressor; it must be demanded by the oppressed."
— Martin Luther King Jr.

A worldview is the lens through which one sees and interprets reality; feminists, white supremacists, capitalists, and evangelicals all have one. They believe their view is "right" and all others are wrong, and they are prepared to go to war to defend their worldview or impose it on others.

The *very* first story in Genesis 4 after the Fall is Cain killing his brother Abel because he was angry. God's advice to us is the same as it was to Cain: "But if you do not do what is right, sin is crouching at your door; it desires to have you, but you must rule over it" (Genesis 4:7b).

The enemy hates Your diverse creation, Lord. His strategy is always the same: steal, kill, destroy. You call us to give, bless, and create. Help us be Your people.

94

Lord, we are not interested in symbolic gestures only. We need changed hearts and minds that lead to Your love and justice.

I cannot hold those around me to a higher standard than I am willing to impose upon myself.

The Church should always take the world's standard and do more. While the world takes a knee, we should be on our face.

Lord, give us strategies that will affect societal change one life at a time—starting with mine.

There was a day when leaders were trained in the Church and went out to the world. Now they are trained in the world and then come to the church, and there is a big difference.

As we take a knee to symbolize the need for change, may we also remember to take two knees to call out to the Lord for mercy.

Is it consistent to hold officials and company presidents accountable for diversity but not to do the same to our church leaders?

We want people to live together, work together, learn together, march together, protest together, but we are not as passionate about them all worshiping together? There is something wrong with that thinking.

When companies say they cannot find enough good people to diversify their workforce, we say, "Nonsense. Be more diligent. They are out there." The same should be true for diversifying the church—*all* churches.

The church's worship experience must be diverse in all settings or else we are asking the world to do something we refuse to do. Any church that exists to maintain the culture of one group or ideology is flawed.

What we have seen on our streets is what we should see in the church: "After this I looked, and there before me was a great multitude that no one could count, from every nation, tribe, people and language" (Revelation 7:9).

If ethics cannot be "taught," then why try to teach your children about right and wrong before they have a conversion experience? Point is: Ethics can be taught or more importantly, a process by which ethical decisions consistent with one's values can be learned.

Time to stop crossing the road to avoid those in pain. Do what you can with what you have to bring healing to those in need.

Jesus emptied Himself and came to serve. That's a good pattern for you to follow.

Talk, talk, talk. You listen to talk TV, you listen to preaching, you visit with friends in person or through social media, and you talk. Your world is so full of talk that you start to think talking is doing—but it's not. Less talk; more walk.

What if you had a friend and they talked about the same thing every time you got together? Does that describe your prayer life?

Stop demanding that God give you multiple confirmations to do something as simple as paint a picture or write a poem; that's not faith, that's hardness of heart.

Leave your current support group that helps you go nowhere and establish a new one that will help you go somewhere.

Time to emerge from your cave of anonymity into the sunlight of creativity.

How can God give you more to do when you delay doing the last assignment He gave you to do?

If you are waiting for things to "calm down" before you create, you will be waiting a long time. Stop hiding behind current affairs as an excuse for why you are not painting, rhyming, writing, building, or structuring your business.

Have you run out of excuses yet as to why you are not being creative? Are you ready to produce instead of excuse?

"Well done, good and faithful servant" implies something is being done, not that you have believed the correct doctrine. If you want to hear those words, you have to produce some fruit and good deeds.

Lord, I have much to do today, and I am counting on Your help to keep me focused and creative.

If your version of God cannot provide for you in this hour, then you need to get an updated version. Time to upgrade your faith software.

Jesus did good but men questioned what right He had to do it. People will ask you the same. When they do, just tell them Jesus sent you.

Stop whining and start winning.

God won't part the water for you until you get to its shores and your enemies are at your back. Then He will show Himself strong. You go as far as you can go and God will make a way to take you all the way.

YOU: But what if my idea is not from You?
GOD: Who else would it be from?
YOU: Well, the devil or maybe my own sinful heart?
GOD: Fear not, for I am with you.

Where God guides,
He provides.
When it's God's will,
it's God's bill.

YOU: God, give me the money and I will obey.
GOD: You obey, and I will give you the money.

Stop fretting over what you don't have today and make plans for what God has promised to give you tomorrow.

You create the need and then God supplies. If you insist that God fill in all the blanks before you act, you are only walking in the certainty of what you can see and not in faith.

If you expect God to give you a full explanation of how everything is going to work out before you act in faith, then He needs to apologize to Abraham, who He told to move out and later showed him where he was to go.

The world is waiting not for who you think you should be but for who God created you to be. Stop hiding behind false humility and fear.

God will show Himself strong on your behalf; will you show yourself strong on His?

If you gave your life to the Lord, then why are you still protecting it by not doing what's in your heart to do?

This is a time to expand and move forward, not shrink back. God can provide for your purpose plans even in a pandemic.

Beethoven wrote for a future generation and stopped composing for his because not many understood or liked what he was doing. Stop waiting for a standing ovation and produce what's in your heart.

Yes, your heart was wicked, but God has given you a new heart. The very fact you are concerned you could do the wrong thing is confirmation of that new heart. No need to fear the new thing that is in your heart to do.

Purpose is the only thing in life that is too good to be true, but it's true. You get to do what you love as often as you have faith to do it.

Jesus commended Mary when she poured the oil on His head and promised that what she had done would be commemorated. She did not preach or teach but instead poured out what was most valuable to her upon Him while those watching grumbled. Pour out who you are on Him.

Your purpose is a set of spiritual fingerprints that belongs only to you. When you touch something, you should leave a mark no one else can produce quite like you.

God is the God of life, not boredom, but He uses boredom to tell you it's time to move on to find life.

I have invested a lot of time and money into my own development. That's why I can say, "Put me in, Coach" and that's why He can have confidence to put me in.

Esther was beautiful and when she was discovered, she was sent to school for a year to become more beautiful. God wants to make you more of who you are, not less.

I once complained to the Lord that not enough people were buying my books. His answer: "Who said you have to sell them?" That changed my perspective on my creativity. I create to bless others and share my testimonies, and if the profits come, that's good. If not, no problem. I keep writing.

"More of Him, less of me" is true in your selfless service to others, but when it comes to the gift He gave you, more of you is required if people are to receive more of Him from and through you.

Lamentations 3:22-23 — "The steadfast love of the Lord never ceases; his mercies never come to an end; they are new every morning; great is your faithfulness" (NAS).

People who get power but have not prepared for that power will be as bad or worse than those they replace. Good intentions do not matter where leadership power is concerned.

Church becomes a ritual when you lose track of why you're going or when it makes you feel like you have done something to please God. Church is not for Him; it's for you.

You can make a difference today but only if you have the courage to be who you are, to say what you think, and to listen to the heart of others. Let love lead you.

Complacency is a tranquilizer that deadens you to the fact you are not guaranteed tomorrow.

Lord, I present myself for duty this week to inspire, instruct, direct, console, encourage, challenge, or confront others as You direct.

My life's scoreboard clock is ticking down. I can see it moving, but can't make out how much time is left until the final buzzer. That is why I live life with the urgency of a two-minute drill.

So the will of God for you is to eat, sleep, breed, not to do bad things, and go to church? That's it? Really? You were created for more than that. What is it?

Since rivers of living water flow from me, it is impossible to have writer's block. Only fear can dam up the Spirit's waters. Confront your fear and you will find your life and creative flow.

First you were too young, now you're too old. The kids needed you, now the grandkids need you. You were too busy at work, now you are consumed with anxiety over current affairs. Don't worry, for in a few more years, you won't need any more excuses because you won't be here.

When you know the truth of who you are and what you are created to do, it will set you free. Are you free?

The same Spirit who raised Christ from the dead dwells in you. It is not a replica or a portion but the same Spirit. What difference should that make in your life, purpose, and work today?

David did not have a word from the Lord to go after Goliath; he made an assessment based on his experience and had faith God would go with him.

My prayer today is "Put me In, Coach." I would rather risk going too far than not far enough.

Perfectionism is not a spiritual gift.

Lord, may the power of the Resurrection be present in my work, words, and wit today.

Acting in faith always involves risk, but so does not acting at all.

Lord, I can do all things through You, so I am trusting that today I can get all the things done I need to do.

When you are afraid, it seems that making no decision is the safest path. Yet when you make no decision, you have actually made a decision not to decide. Where is fear causing you to be decisively indecisive?

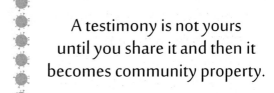

A testimony is not yours until you share it and then it becomes community property.

Religion deadens your senses and feelings, causing you to follow rules and rituals. Spirituality quickens your senses, which means you feel pain—your own and that of others. That is why people choose religion for it allows them to avoid painful realities.

Lord, I am not guaranteed tomorrow so help me make today all it can be in You.

No one is ever a complete failure for they may serve as a horrible example for others to learn from.

David learned more about leadership from Saul than anyone else; he learned how not to lead. God will put you in a bad situation to learn. Make sure you don't replicate it when you lead.

Stop dismissing your perfectionism as just a bad habit; it is more than that. It is a means of protecting yourself from criticism and failure. It's time for you to unveil who you are and what God has given you to do.

You don't need to hear another sermon; you need to preach one yourself, or better yet, you need to act on one you heard that spoke to you.

This week, shut down your excuse-making machine and crank up your opportunity-taking one.

God, help me say more with less words. Help me do more with less time. Help me reach more people with less effort.

The world is listening for and trying to find your voice. No time to hide in a cave; "Put me In, Coach."

Stop talking yourself out of what's in your heart; try talking yourself into it.

Because we are afraid to ask for too much, we often ask for too little.

If you think small, you make God small in your mind, too. Time to think bigger thoughts.

God will provide for your needs and that includes not only your daily bread but also what you need to fulfill your purpose.

What disciplines or practices have you established through the pandemic that will make a difference in the lives of others?

Don't form a belief and then look for verses to prove it; read the verses and form your belief around them.

What if God doesn't want to change what you think needs changed, but instead wants to develop what you don't want to develop?

Your purpose is not your cross; it's your joy. Your cross may be where and with whom you fulfill your purpose.

The disciples were certain they could not feed the multitudes with what they had, but Jesus changed their thinking to show what they had would always be enough. Where is your focus? On what you don't have or what you have in Him?

You have often said numbers aren't important, but then you won't do something because not many see or read it.

Go where you are celebrated for it is God's way of telling you that you are where you need to be.

How many times are you going to edit what you want to publish, broadcast, launch, make, or preach? Time to put yourself out there and do it.

God does not promote people with potential, only those who have developed their potential. "Put me In, Coach."

You don't need a theology of inaction that uses God as an excuse for your inactivity or lack of fruit.

2 Corinthians 6:1: "As God's co-workers we urge you not to receive God's grace in vain." This verse tells us two things: we are God's work partners, but we can misuse His grace and not get the job done. Are you wasting God's grace?

To be good at anything, you have to be willing to be bad at it for a season.

When they needed him to step up, Israel found Saul hiding in the baggage. Are you hiding in any baggage from your past?

God is not in the boredom; He is only in the joy and love.

Why do you keep searching the media for good news and encouragement? Good news can only be found in the headlines of heaven.

Big anointing comes from big preparation. God cannot anoint your ignorance or sloppiness.

"Less of me and more love for and service to others." Now that's a prayer God will answer.

Stop commenting and obsessing on what other people are doing or saying and start commenting on what God is doing in your life.

"More of Him, less of me" sounds spiritual, but it's a copout. How can people see more of Him through you if there is no you to see?

Are you addicted to outrage, worry, or perfection? All those are your defenses and excuses that keep you from progressing in the things God has given you to do.

Time to eliminate the drama in your life so you can fulfill your purpose and be creative.

The reason you must publish/testify/paint/sculpt/speak/rhyme/ compose/encourage/teach/sing/cook/sew/plant/go/bless is because you have a perspective/gifts/experience/insight/wisdom/love no one else has. Who you are is unique, so stop talking yourself out of your purpose.

I often pray "Put me In, Coach" but that means I'm ready for Coach to say, "Not now. Back on the bench." Play or sit, I'm ready!

Your daily routine is not sacred, so don't be upset when the Sacred interrupts it.

If you commit a crime, make sure you don't leave any hair/saliva/skin/prints/body parts behind, because if you do, they can use them to identify you. If you are that unique, why are you trying to fit in and be like everyone else?

You have fingerprints that distinguish you from every other person on the planet. What's more, your prints are not recycled from the past. There has never been anyone like you on earth.

In the movies when a prisoner escaped, they would bring out dogs to track them, for the dogs could distinguish the prisoner's scent. You are distinct, even in the odor you leave behind.

You will speak at least one sentence today that has *never* before been spoken by anyone. That is how unique you are.

Trying to be like everyone else is a futile, frustrating effort, for God will not allow it to happen. Don't try to fit in. You can't.

Lord, this week my path will be strewn with opportunities— give me eyes to see them.

Lord, make me sensitive to the opportunities I have this week to impact, equip, bless, and challenge Your people.

Don't confuse your job with your purpose. Your job gives you money, your purpose gives you joy. To combine them both is a gift.

"God, I'll do whatever You want—as long as it's in my country, in my state, in my region, in my city, in my neighborhood, in my church, in my church on Sunday or Wednesday nights (unless my kids have sports practice), and only with people who look or think like me. But here I am, Lord, use me!"

Oh, how I wish good preaching and services could help us in this hour, but they won't. What we need is bold action, not bold preaching.

Your enemies don't show up until you start expressing your purpose, so in a sense they help you know you are on the right path.

Jesus wants you to transition from focusing on your deep needs to doing good deeds. Time for producing instead of consuming.

You have built fortifications to maintain the status quo, but if you don't take them down, it will become the status woe. Time to move on.

Lord, I want to design my encounters with others so their breath will be taken away by Your presence. That includes books, classes, social media, preaching, teaching, coaching, counseling. Don't "Put me In, Coach" unless I can startle people with Your love and purpose for them.

Revelation 21:5: "Behold I make all things new." So why are you looking for and holding on to the old? Your resistance to change is really a battle with God, and you know you will lose that fight.

Thus saith the Lord; "Don't be in a rush to return to the past, for you will waste your time looking for what no longer exists. Time to move on."

I work every day to keep my mind sharp and to get better at what I do so God can use me. "Put me In, Coach," but if the day comes I am no longer able to help others, then take me out, Coach.

If I live another ten years, I have 3,650 days left. I refuse to waste even one of them but will squeeze as much joy and purpose as possible into and out of each one.

Few ever die of hard work, but many die of boredom and lack of purpose. "Put me in, Coach" and keep me in the game as long as possible.

I don't want to watch the news, I want to broadcast the news—good news, that is— that God has a purpose for you, something only you can do, something only you can be.

If my calculations are correct, soon I will be sleeping for a very long time and can then rest. Jesus said to work while it is day for night is coming. Right now, it's still daytime for me.

God cannot help you with low self-esteem if you have earned it. The only way out is to serve others instead of insisting they serve you.

Acts 19:15: "The evil spirits said, 'Jesus I know, and Paul I am getting to know, but who are you?'" The spirits assaulted those men who tried to mess with them because the spirits were not familiar with them. Don't play with spiritual things and expect to see results.

Build the kind of reputation in heaven that the angels want to stop and see what you are doing, read what you are writing, watch how you are creating.

What is your vision for your life? What do you see yourself doing in five, ten, fifteen years? Where are you? Who are you with?

Booker T. Washington, Harriett Tubman, Sojourner Truth, and Frederick Douglas all played a role in changing America, but their Christian worldview and faith were the foundation for their actions. A cause not grounded in the proper theology is destined to fail.

You are the instrument the Lord plays to attract, inspire, instruct, or comfort others. Make sure you stay in tune.

Abraham was going to sacrifice Isaac but told his servants, "We will worship and then *we* will return to you." You need "we will return" kind of faith.

African American scientist George Washington Carver changed America right after the Civil War when he prayed for God to show him the secrets in the peanut. He found more than 300 uses along with 119 uses for the sweet potato. What are you praying about?

Booker T. Washington, founder of Tuskegee institute, was asked if he ever took a vacation. His reply was, "Why would I stop doing what I love to do nothing?" That is the power of purpose. Until you find it, you won't know what he is talking about.

It's good to wait on the Lord, just make sure He's not waiting on you.

Today it's a pandemic, tomorrow it's arthritis, after that it's rigor mortis. You're right, if you stall long enough, you won't ever have to do anything that may lead to failure or success.

Saying what you will do one day is a sedative that lulls you to sleep where you can substitute dreams for reality.

Nehemiah said in his prayers, "Remember me, Lord, remember me for the good I've done." What good have you done that you can say the same thing to the Lord and back it up with concrete evidence, not wishful thinking or good intentions? Be specific.

If you have had multiple confirmations of God's direction for your life, don't brag about it if you still haven't acted to fulfill what you heard.

Like Moses, you can come up with any number of good excuses why you can't do what's before you to do. Use your creativity to find how to do God's will, not to find reasons why you cannot.

Waiting on the Lord for His will is spiritual, being passive once you find it is not.

Jesus said no one who loves family more than Him is worthy of Him. Don't use your family as an excuse for why you cannot do God's will right now.

Failure is like an expensive steak dinner. You paid a high price for it, so make sure you get the most out of it.

"Just don't give up trying to do what you really want to do. Where there is love and inspiration, I don't think you can go wrong." — Ella Fitzgerald

Lord, the clock is ticking down on the scoreboard of my life. Help me make the most of the time I have left. I don't want to run out the clock. I want to play well until the end. "Put me In, Coach."

Treat wisdom like it is a member of your family and not just a casual acquaintance. That means you must build a relationship with it, spending time learning and getting to know it more intimately.

If you are ignorant and God anoints you, you then have anointed ignorance. God will not make up for what you fail to do because of lack of diligence.

The people recognized who Jesus was but the leaders resisted him. Leadership is no guarantee of superior insight or discernment.

You are not free to say, opine, rail, rant, cuss, hate, and act the fool on social media if you are a citizen of the Kingdom no matter how wounded you are or how right you feel you may be. Love is to be your motivator, not revenge.

Some people are advising how nations should be run but they cannot apply the same principles in their families, churches, or businesses. Proclaim the truth but be humble.

It doesn't matter what your church, political party or ethnic group says to do and say. It only matters what your King directs you to do and say if you are a citizen of God's kingdom.

It's a trap to think that all you have to do is believe right without having to live the right you believe. You may fool some people, but you will not fool God.

Mark 8:36: "What good is it for someone to gain the whole world, yet forfeit their soul?" In the midst of all the "matters" movements, your life matters the most. Watch yourself.

I came to the Lord through my involvement in politics but since then, God has placed an angel with a flaming sword in front of it to prevent me from going back in. The Church must be a prophetic voice to all parties, not a pawn for one.

Don't form a belief and look for Bible to prove it; read the Bible and form your belief around what you read.

Acting in faith always involves risk, but so does not acting in faith.

Do you have the courage to walk down a different road and see something new? Or will you keep walking up and down the same old path and limit yourself to what you are convinced is all there is to see?

I am working frantically, driven even, because I don't know how many days I have left, so therefore I want to make each one count to the max.

It is impossible to do too much or to get ahead of Him as long as you are doing good deeds—not to earn God's favor but because you already have it.

Your potential is an unknown destination whose finish line keeps moving as you seek to cross it. Your job is not to try and measure it, but to develop it.

You say you don't have time to write a book, but how do you know that since you've never written one and don't know what it will require? It's not that you don't have time (you have 24 hours). It's that you are afraid you don't have time to do it well.

I am confident you can do more than you are currently doing once you conquer your fear that you may go too far.

I am doing what I can to spread the message God has given me. What's your strategy to fulfill your purpose and be creative?

"Put me In, Coach" is not to be a referee so you can judge and penalize others, but to play the game—which means others may judge and criticize you.

Time to re-read Revelation not to focus on the antichrist but to see how exalted the Christ of God is.

Some believe they are God's German Shepherds whose purpose is to bite others as they protect Him and His Word from evil doers.

"A lie gets halfway around the world before the truth has a chance to get its pants on." - Anonymous

Leave your current support group that helps you go nowhere and establish a new on that will help you go somewhere.

The church should be full of change agents, not guardians and defenders of the status quo.

Unforgiveness is bitter, but if you drink it long enough, you can get used to the flavor.

When you denigrate who you are, don't be offended when others do the same.

Over time God always proves He knew what He was doing when in the short run you weren't so sure.

God lives in you so it's your job to make Him feel at home.

Stop commenting and obsessing on what other people are doing or saying and start commenting on what God is doing in your life!

When you mess up, it's not time to run from God but time to run to God.

"Put me In, Coach" to any situation this week in which I can help further Your cause.

Lord, help me not to major in minors this week so I can give myself to what's important and ignore distractions.

Lord, I want to be an agent of healing this week for those who are angry, depressed, discouraged, or without hope. Give me the words, the will, and the way to do so.

Lord, You stopped the sun for Joshua to finish his work. I am trusting You for time this week to do the same.

Lord, help me have an I-can-do-all-things attitude and then help me do all the things You have assigned me to do.

Lord, it's a new week. Help me see all it can be, to have the courage to proceed and the faith to bear fruit.

Give yourself permission to be who God made you to be. No need to apologize to anyone.

If you said, "Put me in, Coach," would He? Where would He put you? What would you be doing?

Our enemy has flooded the airwaves with a multiplicity of messages to divert and divide the Church. We do not need a slogan to place our trust in; we need a Savior.

My job is not to judge those who are doing something, but to join them in producing.

A new you among old friends is not always recognized or appreciated. Time for some new friends?

God does not promote wishful thinkers or people with potential. He promotes people who take action and those who have paid the price to produce fruit.

If you don't provide the witness or testimony, the Spirit has nothing to use to reach others.

"God, if and when I reap, I promise I will sow." God says, "Sow first and I promise you will reap." Perhaps your lack is due to ignoring this truth?

When you do not draw attention to who you are and your gift, it seems spiritual—but it is not. No one lights a candle and then puts it under a bushel. Time to unveil the true you.

An aspect of spiritual maturity is knowing when to wait on the Lord and when to act; neither approach is correct all the time.

There are people waiting to hear your voice, even though they may not know you exist. You have something to say and contribute to God's plan. Find a way to express it.

The Kingdom of God is not a democracy. We don't get a vote, only a voice.

The insight and wisdom I had last week is not enough for this week. I need more, Lord, more.

God sent His Spirit to do what you cannot do to fulfill your purpose. Go as far as you can and God will finish the job.

If you set goals based on what you know and have today, you will not make progress. Set your goals and then go looking for the means by which you can reach them.

Peter and John said, "Silver and gold we have not, but such as we have, we give you." Stop lamenting you don't have more to give and start giving what you have, which is considerable.

God has invested much in you and He expects a return on His investment.

Islam covers personality, Buddhism obliterates it, Hinduism makes it a result of a previous life, New Age deifies it, but Christians are the only ones who accept it as an important part of God's creation to help believers fulfill their purpose.

Just because the world has gone crazy doesn't mean you have to as well.

Don't play small when God has made you big in your area of purpose.

Don't mistake going in circles with making progress. It just makes you dizzy and Lord knows, we have enough dizzy saints.

You can mess with my money, you can sully my reputation, but if you waste my time, there will be war. Time is my most precious resource.

One of the ten healed lepers returned to give thanks; have you given thanks today? I thank You for health, for provision, for meaningful work and relationships, for protection, for insight into Your Word, for purpose, for life.

I awaken every morning mindful that God has given me another day and it is my duty to make the most of it.

I am not guaranteed tomorrow, so I must fill today with purposeful activity.

God, I am willing to partner with You this week to do the impossible and reach the unreachable, but I cannot go or do it alone.

I want to die with as few regrets as possible, which is why I approach every day with a plan, knowing it may be my last—plan and day.

It's not that people or organizations don't want to or can't solve their problems; they can't even *see* their problems. It's time to get a new perspective on your old habits.

Some people don't want to wear a mask to the store while they've been wearing one in church for years.

You cannot keep watching, doing, reading, or thinking the same things and expect something new. It's time for you to step out and step up.

It's not what you do when everyone is around but when no one is around that determines your level of spirituality.

Faith should not be a last resort, but a first response.

Do not mistake rearranging the furniture in your mind for change.

You don't know what your potential is until you start to pursue it. You don't know what God will help you do until you do it.

Don't take the old you into the new year and expect a new you.

Giving is not a lottery or slot machine where you put something in, hoping to hit the jackpot. Giving for the believer should be as natural and necessary as breathing.

The highway to excellence is a toll road with not much traffic, for people (dare I say believers) often don't want to pay the price.

You are one phone call, chance meeting, or idea away from your breakthrough. Don't lose hope.

I had a friend once who was asked, "How much weight have you lost?" He said, "About 1,000 pounds." "A 1,000 pounds?!" came the response. "Yes, the same 20 pounds 50 times!" Is that the story of your life's progress?

You will eventually act out what you think about, so if you are not pleased with your actions or life, the change starts between your ears.

Jesus turned Jacob's ladder into an escalator. No need to climb when you can ride.

Taking your thoughts captive is messy business and requires hand-to-hand combat as you wrestle with your toxic thoughts and replace them with godly ones.

Don't act like you are a victim of your own thoughts; you learned this way of thinking— now it's time to unlearn it.

I have so many calls, meetings, and projects today that I must take it an hour at a time and trust Him for the results. "Put me In, Coach"

Some of your thoughts are so toxic that they are causing you pain and sickness; time to take every thought captive to the obedience of Christ.

Change is a way of life to embrace, not a disease of life to be avoided.

Don't talk yourself into fear and fatigue; talk yourself out of them to courage and strength.

God is not after nice people; He is interested in productive people—nice is a bonus.

Paul was free to travel but then he was imprisoned and could not. It was during his time in jail that he wrote some of his most important, insightful letters. Use this season to think and produce.

The truth of who you are is never for God's benefit; He already knows. It's for your benefit—so stop running from it and embrace it.

Your purpose is the equivalent of your spiritual set of fingerprints. You leave a unique mark wherever you go.

If God was going to "get" you, He would have already "gotten" you, so why would He "get" you now when you come to Him with the truth of who you are and where you're at?

I saw this on LinkedIn:
"I will teach you in a room.
I will teach you now on zoom.
I will teach you in your house.
I will teach you with a mouse.
I will teach you here and there.
I will teach because I care."

The great lie is that you cannot come to God as you are, so you come as you think you should be—eventually believing that's who you are.

God does not have to explain Himself to you, but one day you will have to explain yourself to Him.

Busy day ahead, but prayer, reading, writing, and exercise are on my list. Are they on yours?

Don't set your goal to write a book by the end of the year when you have not been able to write five days in a row at any time in your life. Set the goal to write two pages per day for the next week and see how it goes. Then repeat until finished.

I have prayed, made my list for today, and now I commit it to the Lord as I endeavor to do my best. "Put me in, Coach!"

You are not in a position to negotiate with God; just surrender.

I am convinced after many coaching sessions that most of us are fighting against who we are instead of going with the flow of who we are.

Our job is not to
expose the antichrist.
Our job is to
glorify the Christ.

Leadership's effectiveness is
directly related to their ability
and willingness to bear pain.

*Lord, You have moved in
famines and plenty, droughts
and floods, good times and
bad. Move in these days
according to the faith of Your
people.*

The best way to get a word
from the Lord when you need
one is to be in the Word when
you don't need one.

I want to learn how to remove
the limitations I imposed on
myself and God by confronting
and changing my thoughts to
align with God's will for me.

Samson proves it's
never too late for you to
get your act together.

Abraham and Sarah prove it's never too late for you to bear fruit.

David proves your family doesn't have the final say in who you are and what you will become.

Nehemiah proves it's never too big for someone with vision to achieve.

Gideon proves God does not rely on your self-image in choosing what you will be and do.

Esther proves your past does not dictate your future.

Solomon proves you can have wisdom, hear from the Lord, and still go astray.

Mordecai proves God watches and rewards.

Joseph proves God's people,
like cream,
always rise to the top.

Daniel proves God directs who the lions will devour.

The Psalms prove you can say anything to God and it may not change your circumstances—but it will change you.

Daniel proves you can succeed and not just endure in Babylon.

Proverbs proves God wants to be involved in every area of your life.

King Saul proves the Spirit can be involved in your life and you still act the fool.

Joseph proves a high calling requires a deep preparation.

Ruth proves God rewards loyalty.

Moses proves that you and God constitute a majority no matter how many opponents you have.

Thomas proves doubt is not fatal, that faith is seldom perfect.

Peter proves those who crow over your failure are seldom heard from again.

Noah proves what you do today is preparation for what God has in store for you tomorrow.

The Bible is such a relevant book because the Author is still alive to explain its meaning.

Malachi proves that God pays careful attention to what you offer Him.

"I surrender all" cannot just be a song; it has to be way of life.

Revelation proves God takes on all comers and remains the Champion when the battle is over.

Don't die with the music still in you. Sing your song, even if it's out of tune.

Jonathan proves a high calling is meaningless if you don't deal with family ties.

Esther proves God will even use your good looks for His purposes.

Goliath proves the best way to deal with your enemy is to run right at it.

Paul proves you can do your best writing in less than ideal surroundings (like jail or quarantine).

Isaiah proves you can raise your hand to go when God asks for volunteers.

Hannah proves God hears the cries of your heart you can't even articulate.

Jonah proves God's whale is faster than your ship.

The rich young ruler proves God is not after your money; He is after you.

Joseph proves your dreams can have hellish implications on their way to heavenly fulfillment.

The woman at the well proves the reality of who you are qualifies rather than disqualifies you for an encounter with God.

Ezekiel proves God is looking for someone to talk to who will listen.

Pilate proves a politician will usually choose the expedient rather than the righteous path.

Samuel proves there is no juvenile version of the Holy Spirit; He accepts the young with faith just like the old.

The Pharisees prove you can memorize the Bible and still be as mean as a snake.

Jesus, speak to the storms in our hearts and calm the wind just like You did on the boat.

The Resurrection proves a gravestone is a pebble in the hands of God.

Pentecost proves the Holy Spirit is the most effective means to break down barriers between people groups.

God lives in you so it's your job to make Him feel at home.

The men with Jesus prove that intelligence is not a factor in His call, but commitment is.

Timothy proves every number-one leader needs a great second-in-command.

Aaron proves you can make a living from being a good talker.

Jacob proves you can wrestle with God and lose but when you do, you actually win.

Saul proves there is a lot to learn from a bad leader that can make you a good one— just ask David.

Sarah proves God always has the last laugh.

Martha proves you can leave the dishes until the morning.

Lydia proves you can make a living from your love of color.

Lazarus proves the reports of your demise can be greatly exaggerated.

Genesis Joseph proves your family can't ruin your dreams unless you allow them to do so.

Tabitha/Dorcas proves a sewing machine in the hands of the right person can be the instrument of God.

Genesis Joseph proves you can go from prison to the most powerful position in the world in just five minutes.

Genesis Joseph proves God is watching the work you do no matter where you are or who you serve.

Genesis Joseph proves you can come from a family of fools and still be okay.

Genesis Joseph proves that if you make someone else's dream come true, there is something in it for you, too.

Joseph's Pharaoh proves it pays to hire the right person.

Genesis Joseph proves if you don't give up during the process, God can make you a household name.

Joseph's Pharaoh proves when you hire a star, it's best to get out of his way and let him do the job.

Joseph's Pharaoh proves it's important to pay attention to your dreams but then to share them with others who can make them happen.

Moses' Pharaoh proves it's not wise to take a land army on an amphibious operation.

Moses' Pharaoh proves one bad leader can bring down the entire company (or church).

Moses' Pharaoh proves a big army is no match for God's man on a mission.

Moses' Pharaoh proves it's in your best interests to give the people some time off every now and then.

The thief on the cross proves the last minutes of life can still have eternal implications.

Cornelius proves God is collecting your prayers and adding up your offerings.

Barnabas proves you can base an apostolic ministry simply on your ability to encourage others.

Paul proves every snake that bites you is a possible lesson for others.

King Saul proves it's better to retire too early than to hold on and have to be removed from the job.

Luke proves God may call you out of your occupation and into your vocation.

The Temple proves God can use a building, but He won't hesitate to tear it down when it becomes an idol.

Persecution proves God will use extreme means to motivate His people to move out and move on.

Moses proves leaders should not vent their feelings in front of their people.

The Samaritans prove modern cultures did not invent racism and prejudice.

The widow's mite proves God pays more attention to what you have left after you give than to the amount you give.

Herod proves human pomp and circumstance are simply food for the worms.

The Temple and the tower of Babel prove God isn't into anyone building a monument to themselves.

The man born blind proves sometimes you have to stand up to and against your family's religious culture.

Lord, I don't care if people like me or not; just don't allow them to ignore the message You gave me to deliver.

Lord, I am not satisfied to simply survive this week; I want to thrive in Your purpose and will.

Lord, connect me this week with people who need what I have and who have what I need.

Lord, I don't want to tread water this week; I want to swim and make progress.

It's good to wait on the Lord, but once He speaks, it's time to run.

Don't take yourself too seriously but take God and His purpose for you very seriously.

"Someone needs to do something." If you can see what needs to be done, then that someone is you.

Wisdom is the knowledge of how to apply what you believe to be true in life situations.

Breaking a promise you made to yourself is as serious an ethical breach as when you break a promise to others.

The world keeps looking for you and who you are while you keep running from the world in a disguise. Time to be who you are.

If you think it doesn't matter if you say, sing, create, or do what's in your heart, you will find plenty of excuses not to do it.

If I never hear another sermon, I have enough to do and work on until I go home to Him or He returns.

Jesus said His followers would do greater things than He did. What are your greater things?

To succeed in your purpose, you have to be willing to go through hell to achieve heavenly results

To achieve your purpose, you may have to abandon your current audience and go find a new one.

Smaller is not better, bigger is not more spiritual. It's obedience, not results, that matters most.

Your comfort zone can be your burial ground. It's nice and peaceful, but there's no life.

The Jews tried to use a political alliance with Rome to perpetuate their religion. It was a flawed strategy. The church did not, and it prospered.

Four people can look at the same situation but see four different things and give four different reports. Each one can be correct in part but can easily assume the other three are wrong because each one assumes they have seen all there is to see.

Saints of old did not die and become martyrs; they were already martyrs and then died because the word *martyr* means a witness.

We need diversity not to look good or be hip. We need it for diversity of thought, since each person will see a different piece of the truth due to their upbringing, gifts, and worldview. All of us are smarter than one of us.

The Word is truth; the problem is my assumptions, biases, and limitations often prevent me from seeing the whole truth. That's why I need the perspective of others as well as my own.

Arrogance is believing what we see and believe is all there is to see and believe, thus shutting out what others see. We label them wrong, when they are simply different because that's how God made them to be.

You must have a purpose; you're still here.

You don't know what your potential is until you start to develop it, so don't prejudge what you are capable of doing.

You don't have to be extraordinary; you just have to put your trust in One who is.

You don't need more teaching as much as you need to identify the bad teaching you heard and then reverse the effects it has had on your behavior and worldview.

Salvation is not a result of what you believe but of Who you believe.

If I live another 10 years, I have 3,650 days left on earth, having lived more than 25,000 days already. If you think I am going to waste one of those days on religious ceremonies or activities that do not give me joy or benefit others, think again.

I have written more than sixty books; my goal is 100. What is your ambitious goal?

You cannot say you are too busy, for you don't know how quickly you can work once you overcome your fear and ask God to work with you. "Put me in, Coach."

Are you content to watch others fulfill their purpose or do you want to get in the game and play along with them? "Put me in, Coach."

"Every saint has a past, every sinner a future."
— Oscar Wilde

My schedule is so full that I must trust the Lord for time like Joshua trusted Him to stop the sun so he could finish the battle. "Put me in, Coach."

All of us have the tendency to see a part, believe it's the whole, and then not listen to those who see another part.

If you are going to do what's in your heart, now is a good time to start instead of lying to yourself, saying you will begin when things get better.

Maturity is being in the presence of someone with whom you disagree, listening, and not feeling the need to correct them.

If you can't give $10 when you have $100, don't think you will be able to give $1,000 when you have $10,000. Generosity does not depend on the amount but the spirit.

Speaking your mind in person or online is not always a sign of spirituality or maturity.

It is futile to say you are going to do something grandiose when you can't keep a small promise of what you are going to do today.

Wisdom is looking at a situation, extracting a truth, and applying it to another situation that is not exactly the same.

You have two ears and one mouth, so maybe you should listen twice as much as you speak.

Speaking the truth in love is a biblical directive, but so is mercy triumphing over judgment.

If you listen to judge what you hear instead of to understand what others are saying, you are listening to the voice in your head when you should be listening to theirs.

Jesus said His yoke is easy and His burden light. If you are carrying something heavy and it's weighing you down, it's not His yoke.

Wisdom is not a thing for the believer, it is a Person. That is why we don't learn wisdom; we build a relationship with Him.

Speaking the truth in love means love is the motivation to speak, not the need to be correct or to correct.

JOHN W. STANKO

"Treat others as you would yourself" is part of the problem because some don't take care of or treat themselves very well.

If you talked to others the way you sometimes talk to yourself, you would be arrested for verbal assault or hate speech.

If bullying others is wrong, then so is bullying yourself.

If you think you can't, you won't. If you think you may, you might. If you think you will, you do.

You are one phone call, email, or chance meeting away from your breakthrough. Stay ready and hopeful.

Try persuading someone only armed with truth without a relationship and you will usually fail, which is the reason relationships are important to leaders, teachers, and writers.

Truth is not a club to be used to hammer others no matter how urgent the truth is.

Just found the title of a book: *We Are the Leaders We Have Been Waiting For.*

Jesus said not to cast your pearls before swine because first they will trample the pearls and then they will do the same to you.

The streams of living water flowing from you should not be bitter, salty, or poisonous, but otherwise they should taste like you.

In Acts 7:56, Stephen saw Jesus, who is usually 'seated' at the right hand of the Father, standing there. Heaven stands at attention when the saints suffer.

Stephen's enemies claimed he said, "Jesus of Nazareth shall destroy this place and shall change the customs which Moses delivered to us." Jesus is still confronting religious customs and rituals.

As he was dying, Stephen saw the "Son of Man," which was Jesus' favorite title for Himself. No one else could see it; only Stephen. What do you see that others can't?

Our stubborn resistance to doing old things in new ways is hindering God's purpose in this season.

In Acts 7, Stephen earned the wrath of the religious leaders but a standing ovation in heaven.

The Acts of the Apostles are really the Acts of Jesus done through the apostles. Therefore, the book of Acts is a never-ending book as Jesus continues to work through us.

God used the persecution after Stephen's death to motivate the Church to do what Jesus had ordered them to do: spread out and share the Word. God is using this season to do the same.

Jesus, You said those who believe in You will do greater works than You. I present myself this week for greater works duty, Sir. "Put me in, Coach!"

Lord, I submit this week's schedule and to-do list for Your oversight and approval. Change, adjust, modify, or empower as You see fit.

Jesus chose you to bear fruit, not to stay out of trouble or to study doctrine.
"Put me in, Coach."

God, there are people with whom I must connect this week so we can mutually encourage one another. Lead me where and to whom I need to go.

Your have something for you to do only you can do, something for you to be only you can be. Where's your fruit?

God doesn't just want nice people, He wants nice, fruitful people. Where's your fruit?

"A good thing that prevents us from enjoying a greater good is in truth an evil."
— Baruch Spinoza.

Faith is not an event, it is a lifestyle. It is not a last resort, it is a first response.

Maturity is ministering to others even when you are in worse shape than they are.

Faith is not a pill you swallow when you're in need, but rather the spiritual vitamins you take every day.

Find someone today who needs encouragement and give it lavishly—a gift, a call, a kind word, a visit.

Faith is the currency through which you do business with God.

This is a season to try new things, not to mourn that which is gone—never to return.

The sun was shining in Goshen while darkness covered Egypt. God is able to create an alternative economy for His people in the midst of judgment, famine, and plague.

Can God use this season for His own purpose, even if evil people have planned it? God is repositioning His people (and you) where He wants us to be, just like He did in the story of Joseph.

One minute, Joseph was in prison, the next he was the vice president of Egypt—and he wasn't even an Egyptian. God can turn your situation around in an instant. Don't be discouraged— be ready. "Put me in, Coach."

Joseph had his dreams in Canaan, but they could only be fulfilled in Egypt. God is Lord not just of your purpose but where your purpose will be expressed. Is it time to move or move on?

When their families were taken captive, David's men turned on him. What did he do? He encouraged himself in the Lord. If there is no one to lift your spirits, then lift your own by doing good deeds for others.

Joseph never forgot what his brothers did as evidenced by his weeping when he saw them for the first time in twenty-two years. Stop waiting for your pain to go away. Allow God to use it to shape you into the servant He wants you to be.

You are waiting for your circumstances to change before you act. Could it be that God wants to change you while you act right where you are?

Proverbs 16:3 (AMPC): "He will cause your thoughts to be agreeable to his will and so shall your plans be established and succeed."

We can be so confused that we actually feel good about doing nothing with our faith when it is clearly stated that faith without action is dead. I got tired of waiting for an invitation to the party, so I threw my own. "Put me in, Coach."

"What about me?" is what children say when they are left out of something. "What about you?" is what the mature say even when their own needs are not being met.

Jesus hung naked on a cross while His detractors mocked Him and had theological discussions about why God wasn't helping Him. If you have it any worse, then you don't have to help or serve others, but if not, then get in the game.

Stop talking yourself out of what you know you need to go, even if it's difficult or will not please others.

The people knew who Jesus was; it was the leaders who were the problem. Leadership is no guarantee of spirituality or wisdom.

For many years, I ignored what God wanted me to do so I could fit in and be a good team player. No more. "Put me in, Coach."

My loyalty is not to the Church; it is to the King and His Kingdom. Because I am a Kingdom man, I am therefore a Church man.

The Church should no longer try to fit lots of people into the few roles it has to offer, but instead create new roles based on people's purpose and gifts.

The King doesn't just want to rule your church life; He wants to rule your mouth, thinking, purpose, gifts, and relationships.

If the sum total of your service is being an usher to direct the same people to the same pews to receive the same offering every week, may I suggest you reevaluate your concept of church—and of service.

God has given the church a time out and sent us to our room to evaluate what we do, how we do it, and why we do it. Time to change the way we do church.

Stop acting like God needs our praise. That is Old Testament thinking that He needs sacrifices. He doesn't. He needs every one of us 168 hours a week, not four hours on Sunday. That is why we must preach the Kingdom and not the Church.

The church should be the most creative place on earth, not with bizarre manifestations of the Spirit but in ways and programs to meet the needs of others. Time to change the way we do church.

I know some church people who are as mean as a bear awakened from hibernation. That may be acceptable church behavior, but not Kingdom behavior.

The world expects two things from the church: love for one another and care for the poor. When they don't see that, they write the church off as irrelevant, and God may do the same.

The King wants His people back from those who have kidnapped them, offering them freedom but instead imposing bondage

168

We must stop using people to build our kingdoms and try to justify it biblically. Leaders are to serve not be served.

People followed Jesus and didn't have a Bible or a church; they just listened to Him. We have both—but we should still listen to Him.

The Lord is saying to the church, "Let my people go."

Why are you afraid of your joy? Why do you think God is trying to entrap you by tempting you to do something you love and then lowering the boom on you when you do it?

Why the struggle? Jesus said His yoke is easy and light. If you are carrying something heavy, it may not be His yoke.

Why do you think you have the last job in the world, so even though you hate it, you don't believe you can leave it?

Why do you allow people to tell you what's in or not in your heart when you know better than anyone?

Why are you content with boring church but will walk out of a movie if it's not good?

Why do you listen to the advice of people who have done nothing when you want to do something?

If you are to soar like an eagle, what are you doing in the barnyard with the chickens?

Why is it that you can move slowly to do God's will but you want God to move quickly when you are in trouble?

You and God make a majority that can outvote, outfight, and outwork any group aligned against you.

Are your prayers being answered? Are you content to ask for a little or are you crying out to heaven for fruit and purpose?

How can I say I don't have time to do something when I have all the time in the world and God's presence that can stop the sun? "Put me in, Coach."

A car ran a red light the other day and almost hit my vehicle—another reminder from the Lord that I am not guaranteed tomorrow. "Put me in, Coach."

Stats show churches spend 47% of their budget on staff, 27% on facilities and 1% on missions. And we wonder why God sent us home?

The Lord challenged me years ago that I did not value what He gave me because I did not preserve it, record it, or distribute it. No more false humility. "Put me in, Coach."

Stats say that 1,500 pastors leave the ministry every month. That seems high, but nevertheless, shouldn't we stop and ask if we are doing something wrong?

The less I feel God's presence, the more I should trust Him that He is with me as promised.

God has created seven billion unique fingerprints; no two people look or dress alike. Therefore, the Church should be the bastion of God's diversity.

Faith is like flying in a fog; I can't see my destination, but I trust Him that I am on course and will arrive on time.

You cannot steal second base and keep your foot on first; progress requires risk of failure and success.

If God has given you something new, don't expect those who are addicted to the old to see or appreciate it.

There has never been anyone like you on Earth, so stop trying to be someone else. Be yourself—everyone else is taken.

Forget taking a leap of faith; how about starting today with just a step.

Your job is not to critique ministry, it is to produce ministry.

God doesn't want robots; He wants willing partners who contribute their creativity to do the good deeds He has prepared beforehand for them to do.

Your job is not to consume grace, but to dispense it.

Try to get ahead of the Lord in doing good deeds; go ahead, try. The problem is seldom we are too far ahead of the Lord, it's that we are too far behind Him.

Your job is not to criticize, but to pray.

JOHN W. STANKO

173

God may not deliver you from trouble, but will preserve you in the midst of it.

In most cases, when you judge your abilities, you underestimate them. That's why you need someone you trust to assure you that you can do more than you are allowing yourself to do.

"I can do all things through Christ." If that's true, then tell me all the things you are doing.

Since God can do exceedingly, abundantly beyond all you can think or imagine, then please tell me how you can get ahead of Him. Whatever you are thinking, He is thinking more.

Fear is like eating garlic. When we have all eaten it, no one can smell it. It requires someone who has stopped eating it to bring it to your attention. Where have you eaten the garlic?

God doesn't need German Shepherds to keep people from Him, He needs sheepdogs who will bring people to Him.

If you were charged with being fruitful, would there be enough evidence to find you guilty?

Your job is not to sit and judge, your job is to go and obey.

Here is something I wrote for a magazine article in 1979:

"In this age of highly technological media bombardment and of intense competition for the attention of people, Christians face a formidable, yet crucial task, both of hearing what God says and effectively communicating it to one another and to the world."

Not much has changed since then.

I spent forth-five minutes this morning thanking God for His blessings one by one; the list was long.

The Church has tried to fight a war with only half its army. Time for the sisters to step up and the brothers to support them.

Lord, this week presents another chance to serve You with distinction. Make me equal to the opportunities You have prepared.

Like Jonathan, I want to scale cliffs no one else wants to climb. Like David, I want to fight giants everyone else runs from.

Lord, I present myself for duty. I await Your orders. "Put me in, Coach."

Like Deborah, I want to lead Your people into battle. Like Nehemiah, I want to achieve something great in a short span of time.

"Put me in, Coach," but if I don't represent You well, then "Take me out, Coach."

Like Gideon, I want to accomplish a lot with a little. Like Peter, I want to touch many in the power of Your Spirit.

Like Paul, I want to write great works for You. Like Elisha, I want to confront the false prophets with the truth of who You are.

Jesus, You said if I believe in You, I will do greater than things than You did. I believe. "Put me in, Coach."

Lord, I don't want a predictable week where I don't really need You to see me through; I want one in which I need You to show up in power.

God, I don't want only to play the game, I want to win the game. "Put me in, Coach."

Faith is not something you try when everything else fails; faith is what you try or else everything else fails.

Smaller is not better, bigger is not more spiritual. It's obedience, not results, that matters most.

No matter how hard you try, you cannot see all the truth, which is why you need to listen more and judge less.

The Bible is full of examples when God had to open people's eyes to see what was right in front of them. Ask God to do the same for you. It's not that what you see is not true; you just don't see all the truth there is to see.

Peter and John went to Samaria and laid hands on those who they previously would not touch because they were Samaritans. Where does God want you to go and minister to those you don't like?

Pain precedes promotion, dishonor before exaltation.

You cannot escape the reality of reaping and sowing any more than you can escape gravity. Is your small harvest due to you sowing only a little seed?

Two people watch the same movie but see different things; one likes it, the other doesn't. The same holds true for a life event, a sermon, or yes, even politics.

When God opens your eyes, it's not about your sight, it's about your thinking that prevented you from seeing what was there all along.

If you're good enough for God, shouldn't you be good enough for yourself as well?
"Put me in, Coach."

Ever pass something that was there all along, but you never saw it? You had no need to see it, so you were blind to its existence. If that's happened to you, then ask, "What else am I not seeing because I don't need or want to see it?"

Why would God create you with joy to do something and then not allow you to do it? That doesn't make sense.
"Put me in, Coach."

Don't try to be any more than God made you to be, but for His sake, don't try to be any less either.

Esther was beautiful. So what did God do? He sent her to beauty school for a year to become even more so. It's time to stop hiding who you are.
"Put me in, Coach."

You will achieve things for God depending upon your urgency to get them done. No urgency, no fruit. "Put me in, Coach."

Stop putting faith in prophets with whom you have no relationship but who give vague, general words like, "This is your year of breakthrough." It's not your year unless you put in the effort to get better than you are today.

I did a word search and *passive* is not in the Bible. Zeal, quick, act, urgent, without delay, immediate, and bearing fruit are. "Put me in, Coach."

Marx said religion was the opiate of the masses and in a sense, he was correct. Empty religion can deaden people to the reality of their poor spiritual condition.

Stop waiting on the Lord like you are waiting for a bus, and then blame Him when the bus doesn't come. His bus doesn't make house calls. You have to go to Him, not Him to you.

Success is not something you wait for, it's something you prepare for.

What seems common to you is often uncommon to others, so don't take anything you see or do for granted. Share it!

If God wants to make you a household name or put your face on a billboard, it's really none of your business—only His.

False humility is denying the reality of who you are and what God has graced you to do. If you can do it, it's permissible to say so.

If one was helped but one hundred could have been helped, that's not spiritual, it's irresponsible.

Don't hide behind your family as an excuse for why you can't do more of what God created you to do.

If you don't have a purpose, then why are you still here?

One man said to God, "I'm not getting much out of my prayer life these days." God responded, "Neither am I."

When you change the way you think, you change what you see.

Christian-ese causes you to say God's name every third word when you pray. Is that how you talk to others? Then why do it with God?

The Lord did not send an apostle to Saul, he sent Ananias, a disciple. Don't expect or depend on your leaders to do your job. Fellow believers can help you, too.

Christian-ese causes people to change the sound of their voice when they pray in public. Your real voice is always good enough for God. After all, it's the one He gave you.

The people knew who Jesus was; the leaders did not. Leadership is no guarantee of superior wisdom or insight, so don't surrender God's initiative in your life to imperfect men and women who lead. Seek the Lord for yourself.

God is a great communicator. He speaks every language, through circumstances, through His Word, through others who know Him, and some who don't. If your heart is to hear Him, His heart is to speak to you.

Perhaps if Jesus spoke to the Church today as He did in Revelation, He would ask, 'What part of *go* don't you understand?'

If you are ignorant and God anoints you, you then have anointed ignorance. Develop your potential and give God more to anoint and use.

The early church tore down geographic, ethnic, racial, and political barriers. Lord, build Your church once again.

The Great Commission has become the Great Omission as the Church focuses on local matters and trivial pursuits.

Your testimony is not really yours, for it is not a testimony until it is shared with others.

If you pray publicly and you yell, does that make your prayer more effective? Is God hard of hearing?

Your grace is sufficient, Lord. In my weakness, show Your strength; in my gifts, show Your power; in my work, show Your wisdom.

Someone out there is waiting for you to do or say what only you can do or say. Stop being so casual about the things God has assigned you to do.

It's not what I do this week, Lord, that will make a difference; it's who I am in You. I take my place as Your co-worker.

Lord, there are divine appointments waiting for me this week. Help me to connect, learn, and serve others.

I am glad to run errands for the Holy Spirit this week— and every week.

My frailty and weakness fuel my empathy for the same in others. We are all in this together.

You are the wind chimes through which the wind of the Spirit makes His melody; stay in tune with Him.

Lord, I am willing to be as public or as private as the roles You have chosen for me require.

We are surrounded by a great cloud of witnesses; let's give them a virtuoso performance.

God, when I strike out, keep me focused. When I hit a home run, keep me humble. When I sit the bench, keep me joyful.

God, I'm just glad to be on Your team. Assign me any position; play me (or not) as You see fit.

The Acts of the Apostles are really the Acts of Jesus through those apostles; it is all about Him and His love for His Church.

Being upright in a biblical sense is not being right, it's recognizing and admitting when you're not.

If God was going to get you, He would have gotten you by now. Don't fear God's imminent judgment; celebrate His evident favor.

God will dry up your finances to get your attention and give you the incentive to move on.

Very often church is only a scrimmage and the real game is outside the church's walls. "Put me in, Coach."

Don't put God in a box. How He worked with you yesterday is not necessarily how He will do it today.

It's time to be less self-conscious and more God conscious. "Put me in, Coach."

When someone succeeds, are you envious and discouraged or do you think, "If God did that for them, then He can do it for me too"?

It's time to release what you do and who you are from unrealistic perfectionism. Let it go.

Don't let your decisions about tomorrow be limited by your lack of resources today.

You tend not to compare your creativity to someone on your level, but rather to one of the great masters in your craft. There is always someone better than you. Learn from them but don't be intimidated by them.

The real test of generosity is how you respond when you have little, not when you have much.

The opportunities to do good deeds today are abundant but you will miss them if you are focused on your own needs.

At this point in my life, I am not as concerned about New Age thinking as I am about old age thinking. *Keep my mind young, Lord.*

God is love, so when you do what you love, you know you are doing the right thing.

Don't tell me what the antichrist may be doing; I only want to know what the Christ is up to.

God is not trying to trick you, so you can stop being suspicious of what's in your heart.

Leaders not in Christ are always conspiring as Psalm 2 tells us; the psalm indicates that God laughs at them. I guess He doesn't take them as seriously as we do.

A friend is someone who, when you make a fool of yourself, doesn't think it's a permanent condition.

Citizens of His Kingdom represent the Kingdom first and foremost.

First Timothy 4:7: "Have nothing to do with godless myths and old wives' tales; rather, train yourself to be godly." That includes anyone who says they have figured out through secret revelation who the antichrist is. That's silly.

People don't give you a parade until after you're gone. While you're alive, you face critics and opposition.

You and God always constitute a majority.

When God tells you to fear not, it's usually because you are already afraid.

Only Jesus and His followers
can speak to some of
the storms going on right now
and bring calm.
Are you up to the task?

There is a reason Levites began
ministry at age 30 and had to
semi-retire at 50. We are seeing
the effects of old thinking in
the Church.

Don't underestimate your
ability to change and direct the
conversation online or among
those closest to you.

If you are a leader in the church
and you don't have a succession
plan, you are putting your church
and legacy in jeopardy. You will
not live forever; you may not
make it to tomorrow. Time to
think about turning it over.

Time to get rid of all the
clutter—on your desk, around
your house, in your mind.
Don't go through stuff
to get to stuff.

Those who have a small
version of God
think small thoughts.

A goal is a vision of
how it is before it is.

Faith shows you the future
so clearly that you can
walk in it today before others
see what you saw.

My definition of excellence:
doing all you do from a right
heart and in a manner
worthy of God

Your lack of progress in writing
is because you want to be
writer *and* editor. Just write
and edit when you're done.

Jesus cannot commit all of
Himself to you until You
commit all of yourself to Him.

You proclaim the Kingdom by
telling His story and how your
story fits into His story.

The same Spirit who raised Christ from the dead dwells in you; not a portion, but the fullness.

God prepared good works for you to do. You don't have to go looking for them; they come looking for you.

"I can do all things through Christ" is a magnificent truth; what are some of the 'all things' you are doing?

Jesus seeks world followers, not worldly ones.

God is working in you to help you want to do His will and then He helps you do it (see Philippians 2:13). He truly is the Alpha and Omega.

"Do not call conspiracy everything this people calls a conspiracy; do not fear what they fear, and do not dread it. The Lord Almighty is the one you are to regard as holy, he is the one you are to fear, he is the one you are to dread" (Isaiah 8:12-13).

'Don't let anyone look down on you because you are young, but set an example for the believers in speech, in conduct, in love, in faith and in purity' (1 Timothy 4:12). If you are to be an example, that means people must see what you do. "Put me in, Coach."

If what I do helps one person today, it is a good day. If I reach one person when I could have reached 100, it is a wasted day.

Lord, may I use my gifts today in such a way that I bless and help others, and become a little better at what You want me to do.

Beware that when you return to church, you don't abandon your personal quest and responsibility to bear fruit and be purposeful.

God is not a passive God and therefore is not looking for a passive people. He is active doing good and expects us to do the same.

Creativity does not emerge from inspiration but is instead a product of perspiration.

On the following pages are two poems
I wrote during the pandemic—my first venture into poetry.

— JS

Sing My Song

The year was 1991, a failed business I lamented

When I cried out to the Lord and said,
"My purpose, I wish You'd send it!"

I did not think He heard me, for my motives were not pure;
yet that day He showed me purpose, of this fact I am quite sure.

As I glanced at past endeavors, I began to see a thread
of similar activities and results, and things that I did dread

to do and be, all things others wanted to get from me—
the customs, jobs, and duties. But You have set me free!

Free to be who You made me, a man without a mask,
who loves people but it is certain, does more enjoy the task.

So I set out to inform others and help them to be free,
only to find that some were happy and content in their misery.

But that has not deterred me, for now I sing my song,
and invite people the world over to come and sing along.

Are you happy in your work and life? It's God's will and plan for you,
but if you aren't, then why delay? There's purpose for you, too.

Don't be afraid, come join the quest, it is surely worth the effort;
but you must ask and keep on asking, and not be a second-guesser.

My days are short, ideas abound—so what am I to do?
I think I'll keep on singing, paying no attention to the reviews.

I Woke Up

I woke up
And suddenly the man in the mirror was older, grayer.

I woke up
And somehow my waist had grown bigger and my hair thinner.

I woke up
And I was playing with my grandchildren instead of fussing at my children.

I woke up
And stopped doing what I hated to do what I loved,

I woke up
And decided to expand my world to the unknown.

I woke up
And decided to devote my time to those who did not look like me.

I woke up
And realized I could live the dream and not just talk about it.

I woke up
And accepted that God was for me, that He wasn't trying to trick me.

I woke up
And found out the world was waiting for me, but oh so far away.

I woke up
And determined I would never sleep again.

About the Author

John Stanko was born in Pittsburgh, Pennsylvania. After graduating from St. Basil's Prep School in Stamford, Connecticut, he attended Duquesne University where he received his bachelor's and master's degrees in eco-nom-ics in 1972 and 1974 respectively.

Since then, John has served as an administrator, teacher, consultant, author, and pastor in his profession-al career. He holds a second master's degree in pastoral ministries, and earned his doctorate in pastoral ministries from Liberty Theological Seminary in Houston, Texas in 1995. He recently completed a second doctor of ministry degree at Reformed Presbyterian Theological Seminary in Pittsburgh.

John has taught extensively on the topics of time management, life purpose and organization, and has conducted leadership and purpose train-ing sessions throughout the United States and in 32 countries. He is also certified to administer the DISC and other relat-ed personality assessments as well as the Natural Church Development profile for churches. In 2006, he earned the privilege to facilitate for The Pacific Institute of Seattle, a lead-ership and personal development program, and for The Leadership Circle, a provider of cultural and executive 360-degree profiles. He has authored fifteen books and written for many publications around the world.

John founded a personal and leadership devel-op-ment company, called PurposeQuest, in 2001 and today travels the world to speak, consult and inspire lead-ers and people everywhere. From 2001-2008, he spent six months a year in Africa and still enjoys visiting and working on that continent, while teaching for Geneva College's Masters of Organizational Leadership and the Center for Urban Biblical Ministry in his hometown of Pittsburgh, Pennsylvania. John has been married for 38 years to Kathryn Scimone Stanko, and they have two adult children. In 2009, John was appointed the ad-ministra-tive pastor for discipleship at Allegheny Center Alliance Church on the North Side of Pittsburgh where he served for five years. Most recently, John founded Urban Press, a publishing service designed to tell stories of the city, from the city and to the city.

Keep in Touch with John Stanko

Twitter: @John_Stanko

Instagram: stanko.john

Facebook: john.stanko1

LinkedIn: https://www.linkedin.com/in/john-stanko-1600506/

www.purposequest.com
www.johnstanko.us
www.stankobiblestudy.com
www.stankomondaymemo.com
or via email at johnstanko@gmail.com

John also does extensive relief and community development work in Kenya. You can see some of his projects at:

www.purposequest.com/donate

PurposeQuest International
PO Box 8882
Pittsburgh, PA 15221-0882

And download John's free mobile app, PurposeQuest International, from Google Play, Amazon Appstore, or the Apple Store

Additional Titles
by John Stanko

A Daily Dose of Proverbs
A Daily Taste of Proverbs
A String of Pearls
Changing the Way We Do Church
I Wrote This Book on Purpose
Life Is A Gold Mine: Can You Dig It?
Strictly Business
The Faith Files, Volume 1
The Faith Files, Volume 2
The Faith Files, Volume 3
The Leadership Walk
The Price of Leadership
Unlocking the Power of Your Creativity
Unlocking the Power of Your Productivity
Unlocking the Power of Your Purpose
Unlocking the Power of You
What Would Jesus Ask You Today?
Your Life Matters